THE FINAL INNING

KRISTY SHELTON

Published by Innovo Publishing, LLC
www.innovopublishing.com
1-888-546-2111

Providing Full-Service Publishing Services for Christian Authors, Artists & Ministries:
Books, eBooks, Audiobooks, Music, Film & Courses

THE FINAL INNING

ISBN: 978-1-61314-541-8

Cover Design & Interior Layout: Innovo Publishing, LLC

Printed in the United States of America
U.S. Printing History
First Edition: 2019

Dedicated to the Spartan warriors of 2014
and in loving memory of
Jesse Long (1932–2014),
Joseph Lewis (1962–2015), and
Nathan Hayes (2001–2011)

FOREWORD

In the spring of 1984, I was blessed with the opportunity to pitch for the Spartans of Greater Atlanta Christian School. As a ninth grader playing on the varsity, it could be intimidating at times. What I didn't realize at the time was the impact my coach, Cliff Shelton, would have on my life. He was not just my coach but a second dad. He was an inspiration, a mentor, and, most importantly, a spiritual leader whom I admired.

I still have a vivid memory of walking off the mound my senior year during the 1987 state championship series. I had pitched eleven plus innings in a doubleheader and wanted to finish that game, not so much for me—not even for my teammates—but for a man whom I wanted to win his first state championship as a coach. My teammates felt the same way. We were devastated by that loss because we felt like we had let Coach Shelton down. Now, decades later, we've come to realize that Coach Shelton was not solely coaching to win games or championships, but he was coaching to make us men, even more importantly, godly men.

I have a different perspective of Coach Shelton than most—not only did I play for him for four years, but after college, I returned to GAC and was his assistant baseball coach for six years. Even now, when I'm coaching, I'll ask myself, "What would Coach Shelton do in this situation?" Coaching with him caused me to respect him even more than I did when I played for him. I realized everything he did was about the players and not about himself. He cared about the twelfth man on the team as much as he did his best player.

Coach Shelton was a great coach on the field, but coaching baseball was just a platform he used to make men out of boys in order to enrich the kingdom of God. Coach Shelton, I want you to know you accomplished that. All the players, including me, live our lives as men today because of the example you set for us. You were, and still are, a champion in our eyes. You won 578 games as a coach, which is incredible, but every one of those wins will be forgotten someday. What will be remembered is the example you left for us to follow.

Coach, I know I speak for everyone who has played for you when I say this: thank you for loving and caring for us like we were your sons. Thank you for showing us the way we were supposed to live so we could live in heaven someday. And on a personal note, thank you for driving seven hours to be by my side when I lost my son in an accident. You supported me in the darkest hour of my life, and I will never forget that. Thanks for always being there for me. You mean more to me than you'll ever know. I love you, Coach.

Steven Hayes

AUTHOR'S NOTE

Baseball coaches are like fishermen—they exaggerate. Maybe it's because baseball and fishing are an exercise in patience. If you're going to spend that much time on the field or in the boat, you might as well tell a good story. This is a good story.

Baseball coaches' wives tell it like it is. We don't say things like, "He hit that ball a mile," or "That kid pitches so slow he couldn't break glass." We just call it like we see it. That's what I plan to do—tell this story the way it happened. You might wonder about some of the incredible accounts in the next few chapters—could that be the way it really happened? But just remember, I'm the baseball coach's wife—I'm telling it like I saw it.

Watching my husband spend thirty-two years of his life coaching high school baseball has been both rewarding and painful. Bart Giamatti, commissioner of Major League baseball in 1989, once quipped, "Baseball is a game designed to break your heart." He's right. The game of baseball is so difficult to win consistently. Everything has to be perfect—the cards are always stacked against you. It's one of the few games where you can register twice as many hits as your opponent, and they can still beat you with one swing of the bat. One pitcher can destroy a team of nine with his arm. Random things happen—it's a game of inches.

And that's why baseball and life are so similar. You don't always see that curve ball coming, occasionally you get pinged by a fastball, and sometimes glory tips off your fingertips. But every now and then you connect with something at just the right moment, slide in under the tag at home, or dive all out to save the day. That's what keeps us going back to the ballpark, and that's what keeps us getting out of bed in the morning.

Every team has a backstory, a behind-the-scenes narrative that only they know. With their permission, I plan to let you in on the backstory of Greater Atlanta Christian School's 2014 baseball team. I write it with the utmost respect for my school and its administration. I am truly grateful for the three-plus decades that my husband and I have been able to play a small role in the spiritual, mental, and physical development of the students we have been privileged to teach and coach there. We hold our colleagues in high regard as dearest friends and family. We have been blessed.

You're about to embark on a journey with a team of young men and their coaches who shared a remarkable season together. It was a crusade for the ultimate prize in honor of the man they loved—the true story behind the final inning.

Chapter 1

WHO WE ARE

They say every girl is looking for her father when it comes to marriage. While I never made the conscious effort to look for my dad, I did find a man who shares many of his qualities. Though their personalities are very different—my dad quiet and reserved, my husband talkative and emotional—they are both godly men with undivided hearts. They live simply, saving their money, yet generously giving to those in need. They can fix just about anything with creative ingenuity, share a love for the game of golf, and, coincidentally, share the same birthday.

My mother claims that my dad never asked her to marry him. They were sitting on a couch together, and he told her to close her eyes while he proceeded to slip a ring on her finger. "What *is* this?" she asked when her eyes opened, wondering if it was a friendship ring. He had never discussed the possibility of marriage during the time they dated in college or their year of dating afterward. With his easy grin and equable nature, my dad answered her question with another one—not the correct one, of course—"What do you think it is?"

Here's where it gets a little spooky. The night Cliff took me back to his apartment, shooed all of his roommates out the door, and sat down beside me on the couch, he opened a ring box and asked, "How about it?" I actually visualized throwing that ring box at the bridge of his nose, and it was not a pretty sight. Instead, I took a slow, composed breath and asked, "How about *what*?" We still laugh about it more than thirty-nine years later—my parents are still amused about their *sacred* moment after sixty-five years—and we often tell the story to the teenagers we teach and coach. They find it hard to imagine such a proposal in today's world where everyone wants to document their perfect storybook moment.

Cliff and I met at Harding University in 1977 during my sophomore and his junior year of college. We happened to be in the same eight o'clock class three days a week, the History of Physical Education. Although he sat directly in front of me, we never actually met in that class. He claimed to notice me on the first day—the athletic-looking blonde walking into the room. Right away my friend Karen and I pegged him as a Yankee know-it-all—his hand shot up for nearly every question the professor asked. I'm not proud of the fact that we whispered, "Yankee, go home," behind his back.

It wasn't until the second semester that I became aware of his interest in me. During a badminton activity class, he kept checking my record in the tournament. I wasn't particularly interested in his status, although we both won the men's and women's tournaments. My friends often teased that he was watching me play. I was flattered that someone was interested but wasn't really enthused about dating anyone at the time. My social life consisted of moving from one intramural sport to the next, hiking the trails of central

Arkansas with my closest friends, and countless activities with my social club. I was usually shy around the opposite sex, finding it hard to make conversation. One-on-one dates were actually painful. It was much easier to run in a pack of fun-loving female friends.

That all changed in February when Cliff's cousin Pam, a good friend of mine, caught me in the hall of our dorm. "Clifford wants to ask you out. Would you be interested?"

I didn't know what to say—she was his cousin after all. "Yeah, I guess," I said sheepishly, not really wanting to go out with him. When my roommate's phone rang an hour later, she handed me the receiver, one eyebrow raised. "It's a guy, for you."

I put the receiver to my ear, wondering if he could hear my racing heart. "Hello?"

"This is Cliff," he started out. Honestly, my first impulse was to say, "Cliff who?" We had never formally met or actually spoken a single word to each other. Now he was asking me on a date for Friday night.

Since I'd been warned ahead of time, the words came out easily. "I'm sorry, I already have plans on Friday." Truthfully, I did. They were plans that could've been changed, but he didn't know that. Just to be kind, because I didn't want to hurt his feelings, I added, "Maybe some other time."

"Then how about Saturday night?"

My face scrunched into a raisin. *Why did I say that?*

Feeling trapped, but refusing to be rude, I surrendered. "Sure, that works."

Later I learned that one of his friends had actually dialed the phone and thrust it into his hand after it started ringing. Even though his words sounded confident, Cliff had been caught off guard by the call as much as I had.

Our date on Saturday night was easily the best date of my life, not because of the movie, *The Goodbye Girl*, or the nice meal at Red Lobster, or even the fact that it was

Valentine's Day, but because Cliff was a talker! He made conversation effortlessly, which put my dating angst at ease. I learned about his family in Michigan without even having to ask questions. He was an open book, perfect company for a shy girl from Oklahoma.

It was over a month before we went out again. In the meantime, I went out with one of his club brothers, who had been kind enough to ask permission from Cliff beforehand. It had bothered Cliff to no end, but what could he say? We'd only had the one date. He wisely bided his time and was certain to ask me to his social club banquet in April before anyone else had the chance. From that point on, we were together. Even so, Cliff graciously gave me space, never making demands on my time. Had he been jealous or insistent that I only spend time with him, he would've lost me at the start. We grew to love each other over the next few months, and in March of my senior year we were married.

The first full year of our marriage was spent in graduate school at the University of Arkansas. We both had graduate assistantships in the intramural department, which paid for our master's degrees, plus groceries and rent. Cliff, a diehard Michigan fan, could never bring himself to call the Hogs. Game days in Fayetteville were more of an irritation than a thrill.

We lived in a one-bedroom apartment with practically no furniture. Every Saturday night we splurged on Whoppers at Burger King and took a stroll through Wal-Mart, always looking, never buying.

On adventurous days, we rode our bikes to school, uphill all the way. Coming home, my job was to coast to the bottom of the hill on North Storer Avenue, wave to Cliff when it was all clear, and watch him sail through the intersection at over forty miles an hour, whooping at the top of his lungs. It was all about cheap thrills for a couple with no money.

The church we attended was right across the street from our apartment complex. It was a loving congregation who welcomed us openly into their family. We never missed a service. The young couples Bible study every Friday night was a particular highlight of our week. We knew when the time came it was going to be hard to leave.

Teaching school was definitely not on our agenda. After a December graduation from Harding, Cliff had taught one semester of high school in a rural Arkansas town—the kind of school where teachers carried wooden paddles in their briefcases. His principal was ex-military and once yelled into his classroom through an outside window, "It's entirely too loud in there." Countless names were spoiled for any children we might produce in the future, because of that one semester.

While we completed our master's degrees in education at the U of A, the emphasis of our graduate work had been in recreation. We both had plans to work in college intramurals or run a corporate recreation program, not to teach school. But as He so often orchestrates, God had other plans.

Finding the recreation market flooded with applicants, we turned to our backup plan, applying for teaching positions. Sitting at the kitchen table one night, we randomly chose ten Christian schools from a list we'd been given during undergraduate school. We weren't afraid to go anywhere, mailing resumes from Portland, Oregon, to Miami, Florida. Within a week, we received a phone call from Greater Atlanta Christian School asking us to come out for an interview… so we did.

"You should take the jobs," my dad urged as he stood in the shade of three massive oak trees on the Greater Atlanta Christian School campus. He had been waiting for us to finish our interviews on a Saturday afternoon in May after making the ten-hour drive with us. "Where else will you be able to find a job together?" he asked.

On the long drive back to Arkansas, the Lord gave us both a sense of peace. There was something about that little Christian school that tugged at our hearts. When an administrator called on Monday with an offer, we didn't hesitate—we accepted the jobs.

In the fall of 1982, we moved to a northeast suburb of Atlanta and began our teaching careers. Greater Atlanta Christian (GAC) was a small, K-12 school on a beautiful seventy-five-acre campus. It sat squarely in the middle of pastureland on Indian Trail Road in Gwinnett County. Within mere days, the faculty and staff became our family, inviting us to their homes for dinner and welcoming us into their tight-knit community. The elementary school principal offered us $300 to help us get through the first month.

We had found home.

MORE THAN A GAME

While Cliff taught high school fitness and physical education (PE) that first year, I was hired primarily as the elementary PE teacher with one high school health class. Unfortunately, there were no coaching positions available for me. I was prepared to coach high school volleyball, but surprisingly the sport had yet to take hold in Georgia. (The following year I was coaching softball, basketball, and track!)

Cliff, on the other hand, had not been looking for a coaching position. During his interview, they asked if he had any baseball experience. Cliff shook his head…not much. Not even Little League growing up. He *had* played church league softball and outfield for the baseball team in junior college, but he hardly felt qualified to coach. Baseball was being passed on to anyone who would be willing to coach, and they eagerly handed it off to Cliff.

GAC obviously had some very talented players. Cliff would be taking over a program that had won the Class A state championship earlier that spring. He didn't feel the pressure to repeat; he was far too green to worry about that. He did, however, feel the pressure to know the game and how to manage a program. Everything he did—literally *everything*—was going to be a brand-new experience.

Immediately, Cliff realized a troubling side to the sport of baseball—most dads have coached their own sons, and the ones who haven't think they know more than the coach, no matter how experienced that coach is. In this case, they were right. Cliff will even admit most dads probably knew more about the game than he did—one dad in particular. That first season, his senior shortstop, Russell English, was a strong college prospect whose dad was a veteran high school baseball coach in Gwinnett County. To his outstanding credit, instead of showing up his son's young coach, Rob English taught Cliff the ins and outs of working on a baseball field and allowed Cliff to do the coaching.

On the very first pitch of Cliff's coaching career, his gut churned like a high-speed engine, but outwardly his demeanor remained calm and seemingly in control. He led the Spartans to their first victory of the 1983 season, a 5–2 win over a larger county school.

"Cliff Shelton learned at least two things Friday afternoon in his Greater Atlanta Christian baseball coaching debut," the newspaper reported. "First, he learned how good it feels to win. And second, never dismiss your players before all the work is completed. 'I learned today not to let the players go until everything is put up,' said Shelton with a smile as he went around after the game gathering the bases. 'This is the first game I've ever coached. It feels good to get that first win under my belt.'"

It didn't hurt that his pitcher, Brad Newell, threw a no-hitter, striking out nine batters before the game was called due to darkness in the fifth inning. There were no lights on the school field, and the game had been delayed because of rain. Only one major snafu happened in that first contest—it's practically the only thing Cliff remembers about his first game. The sprinklers in left field came on unexpectedly during one of the latter innings. That sent him sprinting out to the scoreboard in center field to turn them off and left him with a mental note for future home games—*Make sure the sprinkler system is set to come on in the mornings.*

Cliff loved his team. A mere seven years separated him from his seniors, creating a special bond of camaraderie. They defeated every team they played that season, save one. Unfortunately, only the region champion was allowed to continue on in the state playoffs during those early years. The Pace Academy Knights defeated the Spartans in the region finals. Hopes of back-to-back state championships were dashed. Later, Charlie Owens, the Pace Academy coach, would tell Cliff that the Spartans were better than any team they faced in their run at state.

BIONIC ARM

By 1987, after five years at the helm of Spartans baseball, Coach Shelton led his team into the state championship series—a series that would be played at GAC in front of a large home crowd. The Spartans won the first game of the doubleheader against Clinch County behind our fiery left-handed senior, Steven Hayes. With that victory, his fourteenth, Hayes took ownership of the school pitching record for the most wins in a single season.

Steven held a special place in Cliff's heart. He had never coached a player so incredibly focused. Steven's loyalty to his school, his teammates, and to his coach was unparalleled. In the state semifinals against Brookstone the week before, Steven, affectionately nicknamed Otter by his teammates because he couldn't swim, had won the first game of that series down in Columbus.

"Brookstone had a boisterous bench," the *Gwinnett Daily News* reported. "The Cougars tried to taunt and harass (Hayes), but he ignored their distractions and—with the help of a flawless defense—never allowed a Cougar past second. 'I like it when other teams yell at me,' he said. 'It just fires me up.'"

Now in the second game of the state title series, Cliff found it impossible to relax, even though he was relieved to have that first game under his belt against the Clinch County ace. By the time the last inning rolled around, the Spartans had the state championship all but sewn up. The Panthers' number two pitcher had only lasted one and one-third innings before the Clinch County coach brought his ace back to the mound. Incredibly, he had thrown 230 pitches in twelve and two-thirds innings, and the Spartans were winning 11–7. The Panthers were in their final at bat with two outs in the bottom of the seventh. The home crowd pulled out their car keys and shook them wildly. "Go start the bus! Go start the bus!"

A shallow fly ball up the middle appeared to be the last out, even though the Spartans' speedy center fielder lost his footing and slid to his knees. The ball plopped in and out of his glove, staving off a wild celebration. With a runner on first, the next batter hit a routine ground ball to the second baseman. A quick scoop and flip to second would've won the championship, but nerves got the best of him and he bobbled the ball not once, but twice. Still one more out was all that was needed to win it all. To everyone's disbelief, the shortstop bobbled the next ball, and a base-clearing double sent the Clinch County players excitedly onto the field celebrating a 12–11 victory.

The next day left a defining mark on Cliff Shelton's coaching career. The Spartans lost the third and final game of the championship 7–4, but even worse, they lost to the Clinch County ace. The young man told his coach in the hotel room the night before, "If you put the ball in my hands tomorrow, we'll win it." Remarkably, he threw nearly four hundred pitches in a two-day span, admitting that his arm was hurting from the very first pitch to the last in game three. When he was asked afterward whether he would repeat the marathon performance, even if he knew it would end his career, he said, "Yeah, it would be worth it to win the state championship."

Cliff knew he had allowed Hayes, who would be pitching for Faulkner University the following year, to throw more pitches than he should have. He made a decision right then that he would never put a player's health and career in danger—not even for a state championship. A decision he stuck with for the rest of his career without regret.

YOU'VE GOTTA BE KIDDING!

Exactly five years later, Cliff had the Spartans playing for another state title, and of all things, they had to face Clinch County once again. This time it called for a trip down to Homerville, Georgia, (yes, that's really the name of the town) for the championship series.

In the same fashion as their first meeting, the Spartans took game one behind the solid pitching of Todd Knapp. Jason Backus faced the last two batters to pick up the save and preserve a 5–4 victory. But coming back for the doubleheader the next day proved to be another disappointment. The

Panthers won the first game handily, 12–6 and pulled out a late-inning squeaker to win the championship game 2–1.

"In '87, we were the better team and let them beat us," Coach Shelton told the *Gwinnett Daily News*. "This year, in my heart of hearts, they were the better team and they beat us. They're tough, the best Class A school we've played this year."

Cliff made sure his boys knew they could look themselves in the mirror and not be disappointed with their performance. He was certain they had given everything they had. Still—losing the state championship series was beginning to leave a bitter taste in his mouth.

Chapter 2

AN EPIPHANY

Sixteen seasons into Coach Shelton's baseball career, God spoke to him on a school bus. Cliff said it wasn't an audible voice akin to the Lord speaking to Abraham or Moses in the Old Testament, but it was a very clear thought planted inside his mind by the Holy Spirit. Everything changed after that.

It was 1998 and the Spartans were playing Bremen High School in west Georgia. Whoever won the game would play for the region championship and automatically go to the state playoffs; whoever lost would go home. This was a must-win situation.

In the doubleheader the day before, Bremen took the first game 7–4, and GAC took the nightcap 9–2, setting up a deciding game the following evening. The Spartans lost 4–2.

Cliff knew his team was every bit as good as the Bremen team. He even rationalized that he was a pretty good guy, why wasn't he being rewarded? It was a long drive in the dark—he had plenty of time to bemoan his situation to God as he drove a near-empty bus back to Atlanta. That's when he heard the voice speaking to his heart: *It's not about winning; it's about relationships.*

Instantly, Cliff's mind was flooded with memories of the end of the game—the end of the season. His big ole senior boys came to him afterward crying, burying their faces in his neck. "I love you, Coach." They had all said it to him… every last one. He had pulled them close, one by one, and told them he loved them too. From that point on, everything changed. It's not that relationships hadn't been important before, they had, but he now realized with certainty that the connection with his players far outweighed his win–loss record.

On the bus with Cliff that night was a young assistant coach just starting his career—Steven Hayes. The mere fact that one of his former players had come back to coach with him reiterated the powerful message God was sending. Cliff could barely remember details of the 393 games he'd coached thus far; what he remembered most were his boys. Some players made loving them difficult at times, but he cared deeply for their souls and determined to pray for them by name.

Cliff's epiphany didn't take away the sting of losing. He would have to remind himself what God had taught him over and over again, including the following season when the Spartans made their way back to the state championship series.

Coaches Shelton and Hayes found themselves with a special group of young men on their hands—a talented, tight-knit team, relentless in their pursuit of winning. Rarely had there been a freshman starter on one of Cliff's teams, but this year was an exception. Left-hander, Matt Handley, only fifteen years old, was the Spartans' ace. He was undefeated going into the state title game and had tied Coach Hayes' season record with fourteen wins.

The Spartans were 28–7 as they prepared to host Lovett, an Atlanta private school, in the state finals. The one thing Cliff remembers most about that night was the atmosphere—it was electric. Never before had such a huge crowd gathered at the Spartans' field. The extra bleachers brought over from the soccer field were packed. Spectators lined the entire outfield fence. The roof of both dugouts held dozens of shouting teenagers. Banners lined both sides of the infield fences including one penned by the Lovett students. Their principal sent a letter of apology afterward, but the banner remained for the entire game: "Feed the Christians to the Lions"—admittedly clever, however, inappropriate.

GAC was outmanned from the start. Lovett's power proved too much for our freshman ace, and the Spartans were swept 11–2 and 7–2. A disappointing strike three for Cliff in the state title department.

The next four seasons yielded four region championships and another run at the AA state title in 2003. The Spartans faced a powerful Vidalia team on their turf in South Georgia. The Indians had averaged ten runs per game throughout the entire season.

Our son, Ty, who was a freshman in high school, and seventh-grade daughter, Alex, accompanied me for the three-hour drive south. It rained nearly the entire time. The Spartans took the first game 9–8 and lost the next two, 3–1 and 6–2. Ty had filmed from the dugout as Alex and I huddled in the stands under umbrellas for two days. At the conclusion, Cliff was handed his fourth state runner-up trophy in twenty-one seasons.

"Maybe I'll be one of those coaches who never wins a state title," Cliff told me after the series in Vidalia. It did seem a little weird that his teams would come so close yet never seem to get that one break needed for the ultimate prize. It always seemed like something bizarre would happen to keep the team from winning.

My role as the eternal optimist was clear; I couldn't allow my husband to say such things. "First of all, there are hundreds of coaches out there who would give their right arm just to get to the state championship *once* in their career, much less four times. It'll happen someday, I know it will." I truly believed that. I knew Cliff planned to be coaching until the day he retired from teaching, and I had the feeling that the Spartans would win it all when their coach least expected it.

TRAGIC LOSS

Fall 2011

In 2000, after six years at GAC, Coach Steven Hayes was given the opportunity to take over as head basketball coach at Christian Home & Bible School in Mount Dora, Florida. Steven had been a dual sport standout during high school and was also the varsity assistant basketball coach at GAC. It seemed like the right career move for the outstanding young coach. He and his wife, Cherie, along with their daughter, Kaylee, said goodbye to family and friends in Georgia and headed for central Florida. The small Christian school, and its close-knit community, soon became home for the growing Hayes family. In 2001, their son, Nathan, was born.

Over the next several years, whenever Steven came home to visit his parents in Georgia, he would come by the school to see Cliff. Sometimes we would be invited to the Hayes' house for a *family* dinner with other coaches from school. Junior and Mildred Hayes had been staunch supporters of GAC, never missing one of Steven's basketball or baseball games. They were especially grateful for the coaches who had made such a great impact on Steven's life.

One night in 2011, our home phone rang and I was surprised to hear Mildred's voice on the other end. "Kristy," she said with her sweet, Southern inflection. "I called to give you some bad news." I immediately thought something had happened to Junior, but her next words left me shaken. "Steven's boy, Nathan, was killed tonight in an accident. I wanted to let you and Cliff know." She gave me as much information as she had at the time, and I promised to relay the information to Cliff, who happened to be on a freshman class trip in Orlando, not forty-five minutes away from Mount Dora.

Our athletic director, Tim Vick, who was Steven's basketball coach in high school, and Dana Davis, the girls' basketball coach, also happened to be in Orlando. These were two coaches whom Steven had been close to during his time at GAC. Both men immediately drove over to be with the Hayes family during their time of crisis. Cliff remained with the freshman class and came back to Georgia at the conclusion of the trip. I remember washing Cliff's clothes preparing him to go back down to Florida to be with Steven for his son's funeral. We talked about the details that had finally come out about Nathan's accident.

According to a newspaper article, "'Night had fallen on a rural stretch of road in Lake County when Steven Hayes and his ten-year-old son, Nathan, drove into a treacherous and dark curve where a tree had fallen across the roadway. They were on their way to pick up Nathan's sister, who was staying at a friend's house. Thunderstorms had passed through the area, leaving the pavement wet and slick,' officials said. As Steven rounded the curve, he swerved his pickup to miss the tree, which was blocking both lanes of traffic. His truck ended up hitting another tree beside the road. Steven and Nathan were both fine, but the truck needed to be moved out of the way. In order to protect his son, Steven told him to stand on the opposite side of the road from their truck. Soon after Nathan moved to safety, another vehicle rounded the curve. The driver, seeing the downed tree and Steven's pickup, swerved to the right—exactly where Nathan was standing."

Steven and the driver of the vehicle both performed CPR as they waited for emergency personnel to arrive. Nathan was taken to a nearby hospital where he died from his injuries. Steven's life was changed in the blink of an eye. He had done what he thought was right; he had put his son in a safe place, what any loving father would've done.

When Cliff arrived in Florida for the memorial service, he was greeted by several of Steven's close friends who had made the trip from the Atlanta area. All of them had played baseball or basketball with him in high school. The bond they had made through sports had been a lifelong tie. They would be there for one another—in good times and bad.

After the service, everyone was invited to the home of Steven and Cherie's closest friends where Cliff and the group from Atlanta sat outside sharing stories of the past. Steven was in a fog; his mind was still trying to deal with the devastating reality that he would not see his son again in this lifetime.

Baseball hardly seemed important compared to the trials of life that the Hayes family now faced. Cliff was grateful, however, that through this sport, ties had been created as close as family. He was equally thankful that he could share his faith through coaching. It was his mission to let every player know that relationships were the most powerful driving force in their life, particularly their relationship with the Lord. Steven and his family were fixing their eyes firmly on the Savior—the only one who could bring comfort and healing and meaning to such a tragic loss—while leaning heavily on the shoulders of the brothers and coach who had always had his back on the field.

Chapter 3

COACH IS WHO I AM

Friday, April 18, 2014

It was Good Friday and we were in school. Normally that wouldn't be the case except we were making up a snow day from earlier in the year. I had just gotten back to my office after a wonderful, all-school chapel program giving praise and honor for the resurrection of Jesus. Thus far, it had been a beautiful morning. That was all about to change.

Sitting at my desk I quickly checked emails before my next elementary PE class. Forty children running laps on the upstairs track would signal their energetic arrival. I had less than five minutes to spare when the door to my office opened quietly and Cliff stepped partially inside—he looked lost. My husband rarely came to my office on the other side of campus—my heart automatically skipped a beat.

"They told me I'm done," he said matter-of-factly.

My mind started spinning. "What are you talking about?"

His six-foot, two-inch frame moved a little closer. "They let me go," he said. "It's over." He pulled out the other chair in my office and sat down gingerly, as if his body were wounded and not his heart.

I knew if I touched him I would be a complete mess, so I sat back in my chair utterly stunned. "How could they do that? You've given them thirty-two years of your life."

His shoulders slumped as he sat across from me. "It's over at the end of this season."

So many emotions churned between us it was almost too difficult to breathe inside my tiny office. Dozens of faces stared down at us from the wall. Happy faces of the girls I had coached over the last three decades. Cliff's office across campus was the same. Scores of plaques and pictures holding memories of thirty-two years on the baseball field—thirty-two years at the same school—more than half of his life.

The sound of stomping feet on the gym track brought our conversation to an abrupt end. Tears began to well up in my eyes, and I had to take deep breaths to hold them back. All I wanted to do was weep.

Cliff stood and opened the door. We silently walked out into the gym side by side, carefully keeping space between us. As the kids started pouring through the doors, I couldn't help it, I put my hand on his arm. That was my undoing. I had to spend the next couple of minutes in the equipment room pacing the floor as my third graders sat quietly in their assigned rows on the gym floor. I couldn't let them see me crying.

Finally, with a deep breath, I pushed myself out of the equipment room with a smile on my face, hiding a deep and grievous wound. A few children read my face, and I quickly avoided their eyes. If anyone dared to ask, "Coachy, are you all right?" I would no doubt crumble on the floor at their feet. My teaching assistant's eyes locked on mine, but thankfully she turned away and headed to the bleachers, sensing my struggle.

The rest of the morning was a blur. I skipped lunch fearing the other teachers would be able to read my thoughts. I went to Cliff's health classroom instead, hoping he could share more information. While his ninth graders worked quietly at their computers, he stepped out into the hallway and shared the heartbreaking details.

As I listened, the term *coach* invaded my thoughts relentlessly. *Coach* is not simply what this man does; it is *who* he is. *How will he ever get past this?* I wondered.

THE DAY BEFORE

Thursday, April 17…

It was close to ten o'clock at night, and Cliff had yet to come home from a game at Lovett, a region opponent near downtown Atlanta. Watching for his truck I walked up the cul-de-sac with our dog, Boomer, in tow.

Most people don't realize how long a coach's day can be. I've often heard the saying, "It's hard to be a coach's wife." For some wives, I'm sure it is difficult giving up their husbands for months at a time to a bunch of boys playing ball. Even when they *are* home during the season, coaches' minds are often elsewhere tweaking a lineup or planning the next practice session. Coaching a sport can be all-consuming. Of course, if it's hard being a coach's wife, it's probably equally tough to be a coach's husband. Fortunately for us, we've never felt the burden of being the spouse of a coach. In fact, it's been one of the biggest blessings of our long coaching careers. We've learned a lot from each other over the years, and both of us respect the commitment it takes to do the job well.

Just as I approached our driveway, Cliff pulled into the garage and wearily stepped out of his truck. "That's it," he said, a pained look crossing his face. "I'm tired of losing. I can't take this anymore."

Cliff has never been one to hold in his emotions. I tend to leave my volleyball matches at school, win or lose, but Cliff has always brought his games home. Tonight, was no exception…and I'm fine with that. The game with Lovett had been ugly from the beginning. The Lions scored three runs on one Spartan error alone in the third inning. The coaches were beyond frustrated walking off the field after a 7–1 region loss.

Cliff entered the house and dropped his bag on the floor. "I'm going in tomorrow to tell Vick (our athletic director) that I'm done. It's time to retire."

I stared at him in disbelief. "Now wait a minute, you need to hold on. You don't know how this season is going to turn out. Besides, your teaching job is tied to coaching. If you tell him you're retiring now, there's no turning back—you may not have a job at all." What had happened to that man who said the day he retired from teaching was the day he'd walk off the field? We still had eight years to go. I hoped he was just blowing off steam.

Cliff lowered himself into a chair at the kitchen table. His exasperation was palpable. "I just can't handle losing anymore. It's starting to get to me."

There was good reason for his frustration—he was constantly looking over his shoulder. He knew the administration was watching him closely this season, trying to see if he could get his program back on track. The pressure at times was immense, and it made losing all the more discouraging.

REBUILDING THE WALL

At the beginning of the 2014 season, Cliff and his assistant coaches decided on their theme—Rebuilding the Wall—taken from the book of Nehemiah in the Bible. In the fifth century BC, Nehemiah was the cupbearer in the court of the Persian king, Artaxerxes, in the capital city of Susa, which is now part of modern-day Iran. After learning about the terrible state of Jerusalem, the city of his ancestors, Nehemiah prayed to God that he could rebuild its walls. God granted Nehemiah his request when King Artaxerxes gave him permission to travel to his homeland to start repairs. Nehemiah and his fellow workers, toiling under hostile conditions, rebuilt the walls of Jerusalem in only fifty-two days.

With such an inspirational story of old, the Spartans began rebuilding their wall one brick at a time. Behind a storage shed on campus, Cliff found a pile of old bricks. Every time the team won a game, the score was painted on a brick and laid against the front wall of their indoor batting facility. Before the Spartans went into region play, eight bricks were stacked against the wall to inspire the players as they came in for daily practice. They had only lost two of their first ten games.

The administration was quiet—it appeared the baseball team was back to its winning ways. But when only two bricks were added to the wall in the latter part of March and the first three weeks of April, the pressure mounted once again.

SMASHING IDOLS

Cliff and I have been blessed to be a part of a tightly-knit small group at the church we've attended since 1985. In the past couple of years, we've learned to rely on each other for support, love, and prayers through every situation. And it doesn't hurt that we share an offbeat sense of humor to boot. More often than not, we have to switch gears from laughing and poking fun at one another so we'll have time for our Bible study.

In February, we decided to break our usual mode of studying the Sunday morning sermon scriptures and do a book study. Several titles were batted around until we all agreed on the book, *Gods at War: Defeating the Idols that Battle for Your Heart*, by Kyle Idleman. For the next three months, we read one chapter each week from the book and discussed it on Sunday evenings. We worked through chapters with titles such as, "The god of Food," "The god of Sex," "The god of Money," and "The god of Entertainment," to name a few. There were some chapters that didn't seem to strike a chord with anyone in the group, but there were other chapters that hit close to home with one or more members. Fortunately, we felt comfortable enough to confess our struggles to one another.

As coaches, the chapters entitled, "The god of Success" and "The god of Achievement" caused Cliff and me both to take an honest look at what was really driving us. It's so easy to get caught up in the success of a team or personal coaching achievements. We both wanted to think we had gotten past those idols, but the temptation to make that the driving force in our lives was still there—no matter how hard we worked to hold it at bay.

Cliff knew that he was putting more energy and focus into baseball than ever before. It was a natural impulse after sensing his coaching job was on the line. But it didn't feel right. He began to wonder if baseball had become an idol in his life.

After the 7–1 loss to Lovett on April 17, causing an astronomical frustration level, Cliff knew something had to give, yet we had made the decision together *not* to give up on baseball.

The next morning, Good Friday, he got to school by 6:15 a.m., which was his normal habit. For many years, he has arrived on the job long before his teaching colleagues in order to spend quiet time with God. He sat down behind the desk in his classroom and focused on Bible reading, then turned his thoughts to prayer. He has always kept a lengthy prayer list handy, not wanting to forget those he cares about.

Finally, his supplication turned toward baseball. "Lord, if I've made baseball too big in my life, if I've put it ahead of You, let me know. You know me—I'm not going to walk away on my own. If You want me to give it up, You're going to have to make it obvious so I won't miss it."

Later that morning, Cliff opened an email from an administrator, wanting to meet with him as soon as possible. Little did he know his prayer was about to be answered—just not in the way he had expected.

Chapter 4

ONE MONTH TO LIVE

Good Friday

The evening of Cliff's bad news I made one of his favorite meals, a spaghetti dinner. It was the least I could do for a man whose spirit had been crushed. He came home from practice looking no better than when I had seen him in the hallway that afternoon. To his credit, he coached baseball practice after school as if nothing had changed—business as usual. His players had no clue that their coach had been dismissed.

"The administration plans to start looking for a new coach," he told me with a hollowness that made my heart ache. "The word's about to get out. I have to tell my players on Monday."

The longer we talked, the more convinced he was that his seniors should hear the news first. Not that the other players wouldn't find out, but he had a special purpose in mind for his nine leaders. There were only four games left in the regular season before the state playoffs, and he was going to offer his seniors an important proposition.

On Monday morning at 7:30, Cliff and the other baseball coaches met in his classroom with the nine seniors on the team. He opened the conversation with a subject that must have left his players speculating about their coach's health. "If you went to the doctor and found out you only had one month to live, how would you live that month?" Cliff threw it out as a hypothetical question, not expecting them to respond.

He quickly went on. "Basically, I've been told I only have one month left to coach. The school told me this is my last season."

While the other coaches in the room had been processing this information over the weekend, the players sat in disbelief. Coach Shelton continued, desperately trying to keep this from being an awkward situation for his boys. "This has nothing to do with you," he told them. "I don't want you to feel guilty for not winning ball games. The administration just feels like it's time to move in another direction."

Making such a statement out loud almost seemed crazy. What direction did they hope to go? This was a man who had never disgraced his school—a man who was widely respected in the baseball community statewide. He was the longest tenured coach on our campus, the all-time winningest baseball coach in Gwinnett County, and stood at number nine all-time in the state of Georgia. Next season, he would move to number six in Georgia history. He had been inducted into the Georgia Dugout Hall of Fame and was awaiting his induction into the Gwinnett Dugout Club Hall of Fame in two weeks. He never demeaned his players, never missed a practice, and worked tirelessly putting in hours upon hours on the upkeep of the baseball field. Umpires loved to call games at GAC because they knew Cliff would call them by name and treat them with respect.

Whenever his administration asked him to do something, Cliff did it. He was not afraid to reinvent himself if need be. Once, he revamped nearly everything in his program just because the athletic director showed him a letter from a parent. Ironically, that parent came to him at the end of his son's senior season apologizing for what he had said. He thanked the coaches for making his son a better man.

True, it had been eleven years since Cliff's team had played for a state title, but during that time there had only been one losing season. Unfortunately, the 13–15 season had been last year, and this season was shaping up to be more of the same with a current record of 10–10. It seemed that winning was taking precedence over everything else.

Cliff told his nine seniors that morning he was tied to them in a way he had never been tied to a senior class before. This was the last month of high school baseball they would ever *play*, and this was the last month of high school baseball he would ever *coach*.

The choice was clear. They could lie down and finish out their schedule with a whimper or they could rise up and go out with a roar. Cliff and his seniors had one month to live in baseball together, if that. So how did they want to live it?

Before the meeting ended, the seniors gathered around their coach laying hands on his shoulders. One by one they began to pray over him, asking God to give him strength and peace, thanking the Lord for the difference he had made in their lives. More than a few tears were shed as they poured their hearts out on behalf of the man who loved them and believed in them.

TWILIGHT ZONE REGION

The Spartans were in a murderous baseball region, even though only four teams were in it! Of the three other teams in the region, one was the defending state champion, one was the state runner-up, and the other team had made it to the elite eight the year before. These were three well-coached teams with great baseball traditions.

Although all four teams would advance to the state playoffs, Cliff and his coaches had hoped to be in the top two in order to host at least one round of state. Even after coming off of a losing season the year before, they felt certain they could challenge for the region title. But those hopes had been dashed when they lost their first three-game series against Wesleyan in March. They had banked on winning this particular series since Wesleyan had not advanced in state as far as the other two during the 2013 season.

All three games with Wesleyan were close, but a victory had eluded them each time, including a 1–0 loss at home called in the fifth inning due to a biting north wind, which knocked out the power to the field. Suddenly the Spartans' record moved to 8–5 on the season. Still a winning record, but not the kind of start to region play they had desired.

The next series was not much better, although the Spartans were able to pull off at least one victory against last season's state runner-up, Westminster. As a coach, Cliff struggled with how to keep his team motivated while losing ball games. He decided to relieve the pressure on his guys by taking a new approach. In order to keep them from getting discouraged, Cliff persuaded the boys to focus on preparation for the state playoffs. Likely, they would not face any tougher teams than their own region opponents, so why not use them to get ready for May.

In the final series, the Spartans fell victim to Lovett, the defending state champions, in all three games. Due to rain, Cliff and his team faced the same left-handed pitcher twice in the series—Lovett's ace. The third meeting was on the Monday Coach Shelton had given his seniors the news about being dismissed. It was a 5–4 loss with bases loaded in the bottom of the seventh. The Lovett pitcher had hurled nearly 130 pitches, but the Spartans were unable to push the winning runs across the plate. Even so, there seemed to be a different feel in the dugout.

Only three regular season games remained, and the Spartans now sported an unimpressive 10–11 record with a coach who had been fired. In order to finish out the schedule, they had to face all three region opponents one last time before heading into the playoffs.

RECIPE FOR WINNING

The Spartans traveled to Wesleyan the next day, only five miles away, to play one last game against their closest region rival. Cliff gathered his team together before they warmed up and apologized to the juniors for not telling them about his circumstances the day before.

"Basically," he told them, "this is *it* for me and the seniors, and we've decided we don't want to go out without a fight. We want you guys to come with us because we can't do it by ourselves." A fire immediately swept through the team. They headed out onto the field taking an early 2–0 lead, but by the third inning, the Spartans were down 6–2. This was looking more like a whimper than a roar.

During the game, Cliff noticed a book propped open against the dugout railing. With only a glance he thought, *How ignorant, someone is studying for finals.* After that, he never gave it another thought. But something was going on with the team. When he heard them yelling nonsensical phrases from the dugout, he turned at one point to stop them, but the boys were having so much fun he didn't have the heart to shut them down. That's when he realized the book balancing precariously on the wall was a cookbook. Not just any cookbook, but a LACE cookbook.

The Ladies Association for Christian Education was a women's organization formed at the inception of our school in 1968. Over the years, the LACE ladies had accomplished more to raise money for Greater Atlanta Christian School than any other organization on our campus. Every year they worked tirelessly behind the scenes welcoming new families, running festivals, hosting fund-raisers, and periodically… selling cookbooks. So, what was one of their cookbooks doing in the varsity baseball dugout?

A chorus of "stomp their soufflé" and "chicken pot pie" rang out onto the field. As ludicrous as it sounded, these were just the right ingredients for winning. Suddenly, the Spartans were loose and having fun in the dugout. The pressure was off. By the time the dust cleared, they were shaking hands with their rivals and celebrating a 9–6 come-from-behind victory.

As Cliff gathered the boys around after the game, he congratulated them on the win and told them they would be hitting on the field at practice the next day. "I'll tell the JV team to hit indoors tomorrow," he announced. Then with a glint of mischief in his eyes, he joked, "On second thought, I may just send them home. What are they gonna do, fire me?" You would've thought he told his team they had just won the lottery. The boys erupted into loud whoops and cheers.

That was precisely the response Cliff had hoped for. He needed to joke about the situation even though it was incredibly devastating. The only way he was going to be able to survive without crumbling was to keep his sense of humor intact.

Chapter 5

SENIOR MOMENT

April 24, 2014

Two more tough games remained in the regular season—Westminster on Thursday and Lovett on Saturday. Tuesday, I left school midmorning feeling achy and nauseous. I spent the afternoon throwing up and running a high fever. I moved into our guest room trying to quarantine myself, hoping to save Cliff from the same fate. But I couldn't keep him from coming in to check on me and make sure I had everything I needed.

Sitting on the foot of my bed, Cliff read aloud several emails and cards he had received from coaches and players. One such message was sent by a former player, now in his forties, whom Cliff had suspended for fighting. For the first time, he was apologizing for his behavior on the team and asking for forgiveness. He professed a great respect for the man he had disrespected in high school. When Cliff looked up, his eyes were moist, and I wiped the tears off my cheeks in astonishment.

Another email came from one of Cliff's former assistant coaches, who was now a head baseball coach at another high school. "You have been an incredible leader and mentor to me in my young coaching career. I model so many things in my program after what I watched you do as a leader and will always follow these ideas. Looking back on my time at GAC, there were times when I didn't understand a decision you made or even liked, but know that I am sitting in your shoes and I see that the decisions you made, both about baseball and the student athletes, put their best interest ahead of your own. I cannot even begin to tell you how much respect I have for you as a man and a coach…take it for what it's worth, but at the end of my career, my last remark will be, 'I wouldn't have been able to coach and teach baseball for this long if it hadn't been for Coach Cliff Shelton.'"

Thursday morning, I finally went to the doctor and was diagnosed with the flu. I hadn't been able to take the flu shot in the last few years because of an adverse reaction I had to my last shot. All I can say is, Tamiflu is a miracle drug! I took the first dose at noon and was filming the home baseball game from the outfield, away from the crowd, by five o'clock that afternoon. My body was a little weak, but the fever was gone and I wasn't about to miss Senior Night!

A large crowd had gathered at the Spartans' baseball stadium. All nine seniors with their parents were to be honored before the start of the game. That meant an abundance of friends and family were in attendance. Many others showed up to honor Coach Shelton in his last home game. Ever. It meant a lot to him that former players and parents had come back to show their support.

Senior Jack McLaughlin got the nod on the mound and pitched a solid game into the sixth inning. The top of the second saw Westminster take an early lead off of a three-run homer. But GAC answered with one run in the bottom of the second, one run in the fifth, and then put up two more runs in the sixth inning after Westminster scored one more. That meant the score was tied at four apiece in the top of the seventh. The Wildcats, however, would not quit.

With runners on first and second and one out, the batter at the plate hit a scorcher back to the mound. In order to protect himself, relief pitcher, Peyton McGuire, dropped down on the mound to catch it, turned on his knees, and zipped it to second, narrowly missing a double play. Shortstop, Lucas Boudreau, didn't hesitate. He threw the ball to first base, doubling the runner off the bag. The home crowd erupted in cheers as the Spartans sprinted off the field in exuberance.

At the end of the seventh inning, the score was still knotted at four. After the Wildcats were held scoreless in the top of the eighth, senior Justin Lewis stepped to the plate for the Spartans. On the very first pitch, the six-foot, six-inch third baseman launched a missile over the left-field fence and took off at a sprint for home. After rounding third base and giving Coach Shelton a high five, he flung his helmet skyward and threw himself into the wild fracas surrounding home plate. With a mile-wide grin, Justin allowed himself to be mauled by his teammates. The crowd was on their feet, whooping and applauding the walk-off home run. Without a doubt, they had just witnessed the most exciting Senior Night in the school's history.

Normally, the Spartans would've prayed with their opponents around the pitcher's mound following the game. But after shuffling across the infield shaking hands, the sorely disappointed Wildcats immediately headed into right field to regroup.

Coach Shelton gathered his team around the pitcher's mound facing the game's hero on the other side of the circle. After congratulating his boys on their victory, Justin leapt across the mound and pulled his coach into a tight embrace. The rest of the team threw their arms around the pair for a giant team hug. Finally, backing out, they put their arms on each other's shoulders, forming a complete circle.

Cliff removed his cap and began to pray. Emotions welled up inside, and his voice quavered during the prayer. He squeezed his eyes a little tighter and covered his mouth with his cap trying to keep control. This was the last time he would be able to stand on the home mound in prayer with his boys around him. He would never again coach another game on this field.

After the prayer, the boys sprinted into left field for Coach Shelton's postgame talk. Standing in the huddle, they could barely contain their exuberance. The Spartans had just beaten one of the most powerful teams in the state, and they jostled each other like a bunch of little schoolboys. When his talk ended, the team stacked it up and yelled three initials—WFC!

Worried about what it meant, and knowing teenage boys, Cliff turned to his assistant coach, Gary Schofield. Gary read his mind. "You know what that means, don't you?"

A sly expression crossed Cliff's face. "There's no telling."

"No, it's a good thing," Gary told him. "It means Win for Cliff!"

Suddenly, the season took on a life of its own.

It had now become personal.

CLOSER THAN A BROTHER

Gary Schofield came to GAC in 2000 as the new strength-and-conditioning coach. He was hired only nine days before school started that year. He had grown up in Boston, still had the accent to prove it, and talked twice as fast as everyone else. He had a reputation for knowing his stuff—after all, he had been a trainer in the NBA with the

Atlanta Hawks and WCW professional wrestling. He was a young, hard-nosed trainer, striking fear in the students who entered his weight room. Coming to school sick was no excuse for getting out of his class. If you were at school, you were expected to work, just like everyone else.

Gary left teaching in 2005 to pursue other career options. But in 2007 he returned a different man. He realized the impact he could have on the lives of young people through training athletes. During his time away from GAC, his faith had also matured. He no longer was single-minded in teaching the students how to be physically strong; he wanted them to be spiritually strong as well.

Upon Gary's return to teaching, he and Cliff began to forge a strong bond of friendship. Despite the fourteen-year age difference, they connected over their love of sports and hilarious sense of humor. Soon they were eating lunch together on a daily basis and golfing away their summers.

Gary knew that Cliff needed more help on his baseball coaching staff and volunteered his services in 2011. He happened to know a thing or two about baseball since he had been a four-time high school all-star. Marietta College in Ohio pursued Gary to play at the next level, but it didn't work out. According to Gary himself, he was fast as lightning without the skill level needed for college. His bad knees were also a factor. Still, he had a great experience on the Marietta baseball team as their student trainer. Legendary coach, Don Schaly, taught him many valuable lessons, such as practice organization, drills, team building, and how to create a winning culture the right way. Cliff promptly put Gary to work as his hitting coach.

Perhaps the most impressive quality about Gary concerning his friendship with Cliff was his dogged loyalty. The latter part of Proverbs 18:24 says, "…there is a friend who sticks closer than a brother." Gary was the epitome of that scripture. So when Cliff was dismissed from baseball, Gary took it almost harder than Cliff himself.

THE MISTRESS

On Senior Night, after the boys finished their chores on the field, Cliff walked around locking up. As he gazed out over the field, he could see his fingerprints everywhere. He loved the old lady and felt like she was his own.

Early in his career, Cliff realized that field maintenance was going to be a year-round task. For the first fifteen years, he even had to mow the field on a weekly basis during the spring and twice a week during the summer. Once, he was given an aerial photograph of our school's athletic fields. With a closer look, he could see the tiny figure of a man on a lawn mower in the middle of the baseball field. Showing me the photograph, he quipped, "What are the chances I'd be mowing the field when they took this picture?"

I couldn't help but snicker. "I'd say the chances are pretty good!"

He took the picture back, shaking his head. "Yeah, I guess you're right."

Starting in October, Cliff began his edging campaign. It took several Saturdays and some Sunday afternoons to finally get the infield edged to perfection and all of the grass off of the dirt. His next project would be the batter's boxes and the pitching mound. During the winter, he would build shelving or cubbies for the dugouts, painting them and installing them all on his own. Sometimes he would even replace broken sprinkler heads on the field.

The maintenance men admired Coach Shelton. He took care of nearly everything at the baseball stadium, including servicing the vehicle he used to drag the field. During his planning periods, Cliff would often wander down to the maintenance shop to hang out with the guys. They joked that if he ever wanted to quit teaching they would put him to work in the maintenance department.

No doubt, Cliff is a handyman at heart and loves his tools. He keeps a well-supplied shop of his own in the basement of our house. He reminds me of Tim the Tool Man from the 1990s sitcom, *Home Improvement.* Once, on our anniversary, he took me out to dinner, and realizing we had an hour before the movie walked me through Sears to look at the tools. I'm fairly certain that was the highlight of his evening. He even bought me electric hedge-clippers for my birthday one year. What kind of man does that? Trouble is, they were the most powerful hedge-clippers known to man. I couldn't even hold them above my head to trim our bushes without my arms going numb. He was thoughtful enough to let me take them back…and exchange them for a smaller version!

We'd only been working at GAC a few years when I realized my husband had a mistress. I soon admired his loyalty to her and often asked how she was doing. Even though he spent many hours with her, he never failed to come home to *me.* There were even times that he was with her all day long and would tell me in the evening, "All I could think about was you today." Though her demands were many, I never felt threatened by the hold she had on my husband. I knew the baseball field was his pride and joy. Most of the time, when he came in hot and sweaty from a long day's work, I'd ask, "How was the mistress today?"

With a wily grin, he'd say, "She looked sexy."

Now, as he turned off the lights for the last time, he felt the lump in his throat. Hopefully, there would be a few more practices on this old field, but he knew in his heart, come next season, she would belong to another man.

Chapter 6

A FUNERAL WHERE NO ONE DIED

It's a rare occurrence when a person is permitted to glimpse the impact they have had in other's lives before they die. Seldom do we as humans share our deepest gratitude with the people who have touched us along life's journey. But because so many former players, students, parents, teachers, and opponents reached out to Cliff during this difficult time, he slowly began to understand the impact he had had on so many lives.

While losing his coaching ministry bore a hole deep down in his core, God began to slowly fill it up with an outpouring of love so extensive Cliff could barely keep up with it. The overwhelming number of emails, texts, cards, phone calls, and Facebook posts gushed in to fill the reservoir of pain. Later, he would write on Facebook, "Two weeks ago I was completely empty and broken. God has used many of you, through your kind words and support, to fill me to overflowing. You have no idea how much that means to me. God bless you all!"

One of the most difficult tasks Cliff had to face before the state playoffs was the Gwinnett County Dugout Club meeting. Cliff had basically been the sole director of the club for many years, organizing the meetings, taking care of the dues, gathering player information, ordering plaques, and hosting the all-county ceremony for the largest county in Georgia. All of the baseball coaches in Gwinnett County, both public and private, had come to rely on Coach Shelton's keen organizational skills.

In many ways, he was dreading the coaches' breakfast on the Saturday after the news release about his departure from coaching. The headline at the top of the *Gwinnett Daily Post*'s sports page read: "Greater Atlanta Christian parts ways with legendary baseball coach Cliff Shelton." Most of the coaches who had known Cliff for years, showed up at the meeting angry, to put it mildly. They felt an injustice had been done and were vocalizing their displeasure toward the school.

Cliff had not wanted his fellow coaches to go down that road. He stood up and told them, "You might not like what your president does, but you still love your country. It's the same for me. I might not like what has happened to me, but I still love my school." He made it clear that he didn't want GAC to be bashed. Still, it was difficult for those who were close to the *legendary* coach to curb their outrage.

Cliff had mentored one of those county coaches over the years. Adam Cantrell had actually attended GAC in elementary school. I remembered the athletic third-grade boy running around in my PE class. Eventually his parents moved him three miles down the road to attend Providence Christian Academy where he played high school baseball. Cliff remembers Cantrell's prowess on the baseball field and was drawn to him because of his early connection to GAC.

After their games against one another, Cliff often sought out Adam to encourage him as a player. As the years went by, Adam returned to teach and coach at Providence. Cliff reached out to the young coach, and they soon became good friends.

Adam was the first coach Cliff called with the devastating news about losing his baseball position. Later, the Providence coach would tell the newspaper, "Shocked is a mild word I'd use (when I got Shelton's phone call)," Cantrell said. "I'm amazed with the way he's dealing with it. He's a great, great man and a great coach. He's humble. When he's winning, he gives credit to the players. When he's struggling, he's always looking at himself and what he can do better. He's just an ideal coach. He's who I've always modeled the way I do things after."

On Sunday afternoon, May 18, Cliff was inducted into the Gwinnett County Dugout Club Hall of Fame in front of several hundred county baseball players, parents, and coaches. He was also surprised with the announcement that, henceforth, one of the major awards of the Dugout Club would be named, The Cliff Shelton Assistant Baseball Coach of the Year Award.

Adam Cantrell spoke on behalf of his good friend and mentor. He told the crowd that Coach Shelton had averaged over eighteen wins per year for thirty-two years. He reached the playoffs twenty different times, had been to four state championship series, and three final fours. "He is the winningest coach in Gwinnett County history, ninth in Georgia history, and that alone qualifies him for this hall of fame," Cantrell announced. "But that's not what Cliff is all about. He has done so much more for so many people than just coach the game of baseball.

"He's an amazing man," the young coach maintained, proceeding to quote the executive director of the Georgia

Dugout Club. "Cliff Shelton epitomizes everything that is good about high school baseball."

After quoting other coaches, Adam made the hall of fame induction much more personal. "I have been greatly impacted by this man, more than any other baseball coach on the planet," he said.

"I ended up not playing for him but against him, and the way that I try to treat opposing players each time I step on the field is because of the way he treated me when I was on the field. He would take me aside after the games and compliment me and compliment my game and tell me to keep my head up and do all the kind of things that other coaches just don't do."

Adam turned to look at Cliff as he stood on stage beside him. "Those are things that I now try to do." Gazing back at the audience he told them, "As I was named the coach at Providence back in 1999, the first person I called was Cliff Shelton. He held my hand through everything on how to be a coach in this county. He even allowed me to come and observe practices—he allowed me to observe them preparing for the playoffs. He sat down with me and showed me what to do and what not to do."

Over the next ten years, GAC and Providence continued to play each other. For the most part, GAC won all of those games. Eventually, Adam built his program to the point that they not only competed with the Spartans but were able to beat them. Adam let the audience know that Coach Shelton's attitude never changed. Even in losing, Cliff continued to encourage him.

As his speech drew to a close, Adam admitted, "I could never personally repay everything that he's poured into me. There's nothing else I can do except try to do the same for others. And really, that's what leaving a legacy is all about."

Once again, glancing at his mentor, he concluded, "You have set a standard for us to follow and try to emulate how you treat other people because of the way you've treated us. And through all of this, you are the most humble man I have ever met. I hope that I have clearly expressed how much I love this man and how important he is to Gwinnett County baseball."

After Adam's speech, the thirty-two-year veteran received a sustained standing ovation on the stage of his own school. The irony of it could not be evaded.

SLAYING DRAGONS

During the last regular season game, the Spartans had to face Lovett on the Lion's field. Although the region seeding had already been determined, Cliff hoped to keep his team's momentum going. It would be a great boost to their morale to sweep all three region opponents in the week before the state playoffs. Behind good hitting and solid defense, the Spartans came home with a 5–2 victory. Coach Shelton joked to the team, "They should've fired me midseason and we might've won this region!" His boys went crazy.

The Spartans had four days to prepare for the top AA team in the state. The Jefferson Dragons sported a 20–3 record, had gone 14–0 in their region, and were on an eighteen-game winning streak. MaxPreps.com, the nation's top website for high school sports, announced the Georgia baseball rankings, based on record, schedule, and stats. Jefferson was the team standing in the number one position. Cliff had not bothered to look at the rankings—he was far too busy getting ready for the first round of the playoffs.

On game day, the Spartans' bus had an escort from the sheriff's department. When our two schools' basketball teams met in the state quarterfinals back in February at Jefferson, it had gotten ugly between the fans. Some of the GAC cars had been damaged in the parking lot, and emotions had gotten out of control. While both teams fought hard and played great basketball on the court, the air in the stands was volatile.

Ironically, the game's leading scorer that night was none other than, Justin Lewis. After the Spartans' basketball victory, the newspaper reported, "Offensively, Justin Lewis couldn't miss as the senior went off for 12 points in the second quarter to pace the GAC attack." His coach would tell the reporter, "Justin Lewis really played well for us tonight. I'm not saying others didn't, but he really had a solid game with his rebounding and getting some stick-backs for baskets." Down the stretch, Justin hit four out of four free throws and finished with a game-high twenty-two points. "This was a tough environment and I'm very proud of the way our kids hung in there and kept their poise and kept their cool," Coach Eddie Martin said of his undefeated Spartans. "That was a physical game, probably the most physical game we've been in this season."

Justin was known as a lifer at GAC. He had been in our school since prekindergarten. He was without a doubt one of the most respectful boys I had ever taught in elementary school. During our slow-pitch softball unit in PE, I had to throw a backspin pitch to Justin so he wouldn't hit it over the fence on our elementary playground field. While he begged me to throw a regular pitch, I was tired of losing good softballs in the shrubs! At the end of his elementary school years, he received my PE award at fifth-grade graduation. His dad, Joe, told me he hoped Cliff would still be coaching when Justin got into high school. Justin had told him he couldn't wait to play baseball for Coach Shelton. I promptly told Cliff that he had a special kid and excellent baseball player coming his way.

As good as Justin was in basketball, baseball had been his true love since age four. He wanted to play baseball in college and had already been offered a scholarship to pitch for the University of Kentucky. The problem with playing both sports was the fact that he was always late coming out for baseball due to the incredible success of GAC's basketball team. He was unable to join the baseball lineup until mid to late March after winning the basketball state championship during his junior and senior year.

To keep his arm in shape, Justin would throw bullpens in his spare time or sometimes ask fellow basketball players to play catch after practice. The first week of baseball was a little rough, but after that, he settled in nicely to the pitching rotation and soon became the starting third baseman his senior year.

Cliff began to notice how much work Justin was putting into baseball during the off-season when he came out his junior year. The first game Justin pitched during the 2013 season was against Wesleyan. One of the JV coaches had a radar gun on him from the bleachers. During the game, the coach came over to the dugout where Cliff was standing. "Hey, Lewis is throwing ninety miles per hour," he said. Cliff couldn't believe it. The kid was so long and tall—his delivery so smooth—his throwing speed was deceiving. "I'm serious. Look at the gun," the coach said, holding it up to the fence. Cliff's eyebrows instantly shot up. The number 90 was flashing on the screen.

In 2013, the Spartans had lost in the first round of the state playoffs to Pepperell High School. Although Justin pitched to a win in the best of three series, he still hadn't reached his stride before the season ended. Now in his senior season, he was scheduled to start the first game of the doubleheader against Jefferson.

Already a section of the home bleachers was filled with rowdy teenagers seeking revenge and ready to heckle the visiting Spartans. In basketball, Justin never noticed what the opposing fans were yelling—the game was too fast-paced to be aware of what was going on in the stands—but he could definitely hear what was being said during the slower-paced game of baseball. Sometimes it was simply good-natured fun, while other times it was racial.

No matter what was being hurled from the bleachers, Justin never lost control of his emotions. He was a workhorse the entire seven innings of the first game against Jefferson, only giving up one earned run, walking one batter, and scattering four hits. He wreaked as much havoc from the plate as he did on the mound.

With the score tied 1–1 and a Jefferson runner on first base, the next batter in the lineup connected with Justin's fastball. It was well over the head of the speedy left fielder, Connor Joseph, whose first step had been forward instead of back. Everyone in the Jefferson bleachers rose up in unison, arms thrust above their heads, waiting for the ball to clear the fence or at least drop just inside of it.

What happened next left everyone baffled, including Connor himself. Even after capturing the play on video, I still couldn't believe what I had seen. For days to come, I watched that one play over and over again trying to make sense of it. After Connor realized the ball would be over his head, he turned his back on the ball and ran full speed toward the outfield fence. At the last possible second, he left his feet, diving headlong onto the gravel warning track, glove hand outstretched. A cloud of gray dust swelled up around him as everyone in the stands looked for the ball rolling on the ground. But it wasn't on the ground—it was snuggled deep within the leather pocket of Connor's glove! He knew his chin was scraped and bloodied, but he came to his feet with lightning speed and hurled the ball back to the infield, thus holding their base runner to first.

Cliff turned to Coach Schofield and laughed. "Is this *Angels in the Outfield*?" If so, the *angels* weren't through with the Spartans yet.

In the top of the sixth, still tied at one, Justin came to the plate and promptly drove in two runs on a single up the middle. That would be the final score when the last out was made in the bottom of the seventh. Justin's long legs propelled him off the mound as he strode toward the dugout, giving his teammates high fives for their 3–1 victory.

The Jefferson players and fans seemed to be unfazed by the Spartans' victory. It had to be a fluke. No way would an unranked team, and a number four region seed at that, come to their field and walk away with two wins. They were confident this series would continue tomorrow.

Taking that bravado into the first inning of game two, the Dragons quickly went up 2–0 off of four scorching base hits. The Spartans answered with one run in the second inning and two more in the third, before the Dragons went up by two in the fifth. All in all, the two teams would exchange the lead nine times over the course of the game.

When the Spartans went up by one run in the bottom of the sixth, Jefferson's season appeared to be over. Baseball, however, is a game of inches and split-second calculations. Spartans' right fielder Peyton McGuire took a gamble in the top of the seventh, diving for a hard-hit ball. Unfortunately, the ball hit the ground and skipped past his glove. A Dragon base runner came around to score, creating a rousing ruckus in the stands. At the end of the inning, Peyton ran off the field amidst jeers and insults from the opposing crowd. He felt like he had just let his teammates down—his heart was sick.

In the bottom of the seventh, the Spartans had a chance to win the game but couldn't push the winning run across the plate. The fans were getting their money's worth as the eighth inning rolled around. No doubt about it, the Dragons were a great team. They had a powerful batting lineup along with an exceptionally quick outfield, sporting some of the strongest arms Coach Shelton had ever seen on the high school level.

In the bottom of the eighth inning, Justin Lewis strode to the plate facing Jefferson's game three starting pitcher. With their season on the line, the Dragons had to win game two at all costs. When Justin connected with the ball, Coach Shelton ran out of the coaching box and down the line in left field. He couldn't help but follow the flight of the ball. When it cleared the outfield fence just inside the foul pole, Cliff had to sprint to get back to third before Justin made it around the bases.

As Justin gave his coach a high five, he flew toward home with his fist raised high in the air. Coach Schofield had already run across the infield to hold the other players in the dugout. He didn't want anything to happen to prevent the winning run from scoring. As soon as Justin's foot stomped home plate, he turned into a wave of adrenalized teammates, who promptly took him to the ground on his back. The Jefferson fans were forced to watch a dog pile on top of their own home plate.

When the melee cleared, the athletes walked across the infield shaking hands. Both teams seemed stunned by the outcome. The boys of Jefferson immediately went to their storage shed, pulled out the field equipment, and began raking the infield as if they had another game the next day. There were no players huddling together for comfort or kneeling on the ground in tears; they simply went about their postgame business as usual. It was perhaps the strangest reaction to a devastating loss I had ever witnessed.

The Spartans, on the other hand, continued their celebratory whoops and cheers in left field. Our son, Ty, was among the celebrators.

Ty had spent his first two years out of college teaching and coaching as a mission in Rwanda, Africa, and was now a substitute teacher at GAC. He was on the baseball coaching staff primarily to help keep the boys encouraged and focused. All season, Ty had been a powerful motivator to the team. As Cliff and his other two coaches watched the boys revel in their win, Ty worked his way among the guys celebrating with them.

Cliff would later say that it was one of the greatest privileges of his life to be able to coach with his son during his final season. Ty had been there during two of the most difficult moments in Cliff's baseball career. He had suffered losses before, but nothing broke his heart like the 1987 loss of the state championship to Clinch County. Ty was just an infant at the time of that series. Even though Cliff came home devastated, he remembered finding solace by rocking his four-month-old son to sleep while still wearing his baseball uniform. Now, suffering his second heartbreak in baseball, losing his job, he felt comfort having his son by his side.

Ty had always been involved as a Spartans baseball fan but had never played the game, save for one season with the Little League Dodgers in the second grade. His God-given talent was running, and he had used that gift to the fullest, winning a AA state championship in cross-country his senior year and state runner-up in the two-mile in track. He had taken every season-ending loss in baseball to heart over the years, sometimes sitting in the dugout in tears as a boy. He simply couldn't stand to see his dad hurt. But maybe this year would be different—after all, the Spartans had just knocked off the number-one ranked team in the state!

While winning the first round of state was exhilarating, there was still much work to be done and no guarantee for tomorrow. With four rounds remaining, the Spartans would have to face a better team at every turn. How long could the magic last?

Chapter 7

RUN-OF-THE-MILL

May 7, 2014

The following week I found myself driving through Lindale, Georgia, about an hour and a half north and west of Atlanta. Off of Highway 411, Maple Road meanders through a shaded neighborhood of old houses. Crossing double railroad tracks, my attention was drawn to the ruins of a massive brick structure on the right side of the road. I would've enjoyed exploring around the two gigantic smoke stacks still standing guard over the extensive property. But it looked dangerous and I didn't have time to stop or even gawk at the sight, as the turnoff for Pepperell High school, the Spartan's second-round state opponent, was just ahead. I made a mental note to find out more about the intriguing ruins.

Pepperell was a familiar opponent—this was the team who had knocked us out of state in the very first round last season. The first time our two teams had ever met was in 2013, and though it took three games for Pepperell to dispense with the Spartans that year, an unusual bond was forged between the two coaches despite their age difference.

A newspaper reporter once quipped that Coach Shelton is "no enemy to chitchat." So when Cliff arrived with his team early for the third game in the 2013 series, he struck up a conversation with the thirty-six-year-old Pepperell coach, Wright Edge. (Wright was four years old when Cliff started his coaching career.) Later, Cliff told me that it bordered on a spiritual conversation, not the usual kind of talk between two baseball coaches preparing to do battle.

Even more unusual was the fact that in January, prior to the start of the 2014 baseball season, Cliff received a phone call from the Pepperell coach. His sole purpose in calling was to tell Coach Shelton that he had been thinking about him and wanted to wish him the best in the upcoming season. Cliff hung up from the call both surprised and honored that a coach, whom he had only met once, would take the time to call. And now, four months later, the Spartans were about to face the Pepperell Dragons again on their field.

Cliff and his team arrived early and stepped off of the bus into the sweltering afternoon heat. As the players made their way to the shade of the visiting dugout, Cliff was met by the Pepperell coach. The two shook hands and exchanged pleasantries, and then Coach Edge invited him to the home dugout. "I have something for you," he said.

Cliff followed the young coach across the field and waited for him to emerge from the home dugout. Instead of handing him the expected lineup card and game ball, he held out a gift and explained the meaning behind it. Stunned by the news of Cliff's dismissal from coaching, Coach Edge had not only spent the previous four days preparing his team for the Spartans, but he had spent his spare time looking for a special gift for their coach.

Wright Edge had been raised all of his life in the Lindale community—a community that owed its very existence to

Pepperell Fabrics. In 1896, Massachusetts Mills opened in Lindale, employing nearly fourteen hundred workers. They produced one-seventh of all textiles in the state of Georgia. The original mill was three stories tall with one brick smoke stack. When the second mill was built beside it in 1899, another massive smoke stack was added, and the community promptly named them Bread and Butter—after all, they knew where their bread was being buttered.

By 1926, the mill was sold to the Pepperell Manufacturing Company. In that same year, the mill built a school and paid all of the teaching salaries. Lindale's doctors, dentists, nurses, and fire department salaries were also paid by the mill.

At the time of the Great Depression, there were eight different textile mills operating in Floyd County. In order to keep their workers involved and happy, the Northwest Georgia Textile (Baseball) League was formed in 1931.

During the Depression, a textile worker could make twelve to fourteen dollars a week in the factory with an extra four to seven dollars added for playing on the mill baseball team. Each mill had its own ball field, usually at the center of the mill village where sometimes up to two thousand fans would pay twenty-five cents per ticket to cheer on their favorite team. For three decades, a sense of solidarity and pride drew the communities together around the Northwest Georgia Textile League.

The memories of the old textile league still lingered in Lindale, Georgia. While the official Pepperell High School colors are gold and white, the baseball team still honored the league by wearing its colors—red, gray, and white. They were the only team on campus that still held on to the heritage of the old mill, which now lay in ruins only a few blocks away.

Coach Wright Edge was tied to the Pepperell Mill by heritage. Both of his maternal grandparents had worked there. The mill whistle sounded one long, final blast on

September 28, 2001 at three o'clock in the afternoon. The last bolt of cloth finished its journey through the machines before the old mill fell silent, dealing a deadly blow to the economy of Lindale. Coach Edge had gone to Pepperell High School while the mill was in full operation. He remembered the tight-knit community life that revolved around the mill. When it shut down, the people of the community wanted to hold on to a piece of it—the mill was who they were.

Coach Edge laid his heartfelt gift into Coach Shelton's hands. Just a few days prior, he had gone to a man whose family had worked in the Pepperell Mill for generations. He was looking for something special to remind Cliff of their community and their proud history.

"This piece of cloth," he said, "is from the last bolt to ever come through our mill." The 6 x 6-inch cloth was imprinted with a beautiful color painting of the mill. Then he handed Cliff an ink pen. "This pen is made out of the maple wood of the old mill floor." Coach Edge's next words left Cliff with a lump in his throat. "I wanted you to have this because you've made a profound impact on my life."

Cliff didn't know what to say. He had never had an opponent do such a thing before. He was deeply moved by the gesture.

That evening on the way back to Atlanta I passed the bus and honked. Cliff waved from the driver's seat, and I could hear the boys singing, even with my windows rolled up. None of the players ever rode home with their parents after a game—it was a tight team and they all wanted to be on the bus together, especially when they were celebrating a victory! The Spartans had swept the Pepperell Dragons 2–1 and 14–4.

When Cliff came in later that night, he showed me the gift that Coach Edge had given him. His voice broke as he laid the cloth and pen on the table. "I want this to go in a special place in our house. What he did means a lot to me."

I not only found a place in our house to display the gift, but when the season was over I called Coach Edge. At the time of my call, he happened to be at a baseball coach's clinic in Atlanta. I had caught him during a break, and he was delighted to have the opportunity to talk about his relationship with Cliff.

Right away he told me that the first time he met Coach Shelton he knew there was something different about him. "The first words out of his mouth were not like the typical macho baseball coach who knows everything. I knew that I could learn from this guy."

The young coach had watched the way Cliff treated his players with respect and how his players admired him in return. He wanted his boys to respect him the same way. Even though his players came from a rougher background than the ones at a private school like GAC, Coach Edge wanted to make a difference in their lives. "I have some kids on my team that I'm not gonna give up on."

Just before our conversation ended, he added, "If I ever felt like I needed guidance, I knew I could call Coach Shelton. I felt like we'd known each other for ten years."

As Cliff continued to prepare his team for the next round, he did so with a sense of appreciation for a young coach in northwest Georgia. Even though GAC had defeated Pepperell, there was no doubt Wright Edge would be pulling for the Spartans the rest of the way—a thoughtful coach with an unusual name, trying to do things the right way, learning from a man who already was.

Chapter 8

UPHILL BATTLE

May 13, 2014

Our nomadic tribe and its loyal followers crisscrossed Georgia from one end to the other. We had traveled north and east to Jefferson, north and west to Pepperell, and now the Spartans caravan rolled toward Berrien High School in rural Nashville, four hours due south. Cliff had already made arrangements for his team and coaches to spend the night in nearby Tifton just in case the two teams split.

The weather on Tuesday afternoon in South Georgia was typical for mid-May, hot and muggy. The field beside Berrien High School was anything *but* typical. When I got to the visitors' bleachers, the other Spartans fans confirmed that my eyes were not playing tricks—there was a hill in right center field. Not just an inconsequential slope—a hill! During the course of the afternoon, our senior center fielder, Ross Wood, chased a ball up the hill, caught it, then jumped off, making a two-footed landing for emphasis. The grin on his face reminded me of the mischievous rascal I had taught in elementary school.

Besides the hill, there were two other factors that would give the Berrien Rebels a slight advantage. The pitcher's mound seemed smaller than usual. Justin Lewis was pitching the first game, and his long stride practically took him onto the grass every pitch. His size 16.5 shoes barely fit on top of the mound. And to top it off, the Rebels kept a rhythmic beat thumping on the tin roof of the dugout with wooden clubs while chanting loudly during their entire at-bat of every inning. As annoying as it was to me, I couldn't imagine what it would do to our pitchers on the mound.

Justin pitched a decent game but struggled to find his usual rhythm. Our bats failed to rally, and surprisingly, we lost by a score of 2–1. The Spartans were unaccustomed to losing a game with Justin on the mound. Now we all wondered if this would be the end of the road for our boys.

I turned toward the football practice field behind us and stared at the giant white letters on top of two tall poles at the far end of the field. H-O-P-E. That was all we could do now.

LONG BALL

As game two of the doubleheader progressed, the Spartans were flat. The earlier loss and draining humidity appeared to have taken the wind out of their sails. The Rebels had scored one run in the third inning and three in the top of the fourth. Down 4–0, things looked bleak until the Spartans managed to get a couple of runners on base. When our stout catcher, Devin Daugherty, strode to the plate, he promptly hit a home run over the center-field fence. Now the Spartans were only down by one.

On a Rebel error and a Spartan single, there were once again two men on base for our designated hitter, Jackson O'Brien. Jackson was carrying a heavy burden to the plate—a burden that had nothing to do with baseball. His grandfather, Jesse Long, lay dying at his home in Duluth, a suburb of Atlanta.

In the 1960s, Jesse Long, a young man in his thirties, was the founder of our school, the first president, and now the beloved chancellor. Greater Atlanta Christian School would not be in existence today had it not been for Jesse's single-minded vision and steadfast faith.

Jesse loved baseball and loved Cliff even more. In the beginning of Cliff's baseball career, Jesse used to poke fun of his Michigan accent until it began fading into a neutral North–South blend.

When Jesse published his memoir in 2008, chapter 17 was entitled "Key People."[1] He wrote in the first paragraph of that chapter: "The history of Greater Atlanta Christian School really is the history of its people. But GACS history has an extra dimension. We have had a group of outstanding teachers and administrators. Though they have been great, our successes seem to be even greater than the contributions of our staff members. We believe that our heavenly Father has been involved and that He deserves the credit." Jesse chose to include a small group of people who he deemed to be key leaders in the early growth of the school. Cliff and I had joined the GAC staff at the beginning of the school's thirteenth year and were named among thirty-eight *key people* in his book. We were deeply honored to be included, especially when we think of the many who could have been there instead of us.

Cliff also had a long-standing tradition that included Brother Jesse. Our school's annual Celebration Dinner, with

1. Jesse Long, *Greater Atlanta Christian School, The Early Days, A Memoir* (Norcross, GA: DSI Publishing, 2008).

board members and patrons in attendance, is held every May as a way for the administration to show appreciation to its hard-working faculty and staff. We have always enjoyed a nice dinner in the ballroom of an upscale hotel in the Atlanta area. At the close of every Celebration Dinner, Cliff's mission was to go straight to Jesse's table for one purpose—to say, "Thank you for starting our school."

Cliff and I couldn't imagine being anywhere else. Teaching and coaching at GAC had never seemed like a job to us; it was our life's ministry. We had Jesse to thank for that. Cliff wanted to express his gratitude to this great man at the end of every school year. It happened so many times over the years, Jesse would see him coming, and with a twinkle in his eye, say, "I know why you're here." Cliff would smile, take his hand, and say *thank you* anyway.

You could see Jesse, and his wife, Marilyn, in the stands for every home baseball game, especially since their grandson Jackson O'Brien had been a starter on the varsity since his freshman year. Until Jackson's senior year, Jesse graced the same seat behind home plate where he could keep a good eye on the Spartans' catcher.

Jackson had been the number one catcher for three seasons. The tall, slender redhead was a solid defender for the team until he hurt his throwing arm and got sick with mono during the second month of his senior season. Devin Daugherty stepped into the catcher's position after that and never relinquished it.

Jackson could have been bitter, but he was a better man than that. He embraced the roll of a backup fielder and eventually became the Spartan's lethal designated hitter. His one regret was that his eighty-two-year-old grandfather had not been able to attend any baseball games this season. The stands seemed lonely without him.

Jackson now stepped to the plate with his team down by one. He hoped to push at least one and maybe two runs across the plate. He had been playing baseball since the age of four and been in many situations like this one, but he had never once hit a home run—not one ball had ever sailed over the fence in his fourteen years at the plate.

In this situation with two runners on, Jackson was patient as always, waiting for his pitch to come down the pipe. When he saw what he was looking for, the bat and ball connected with a nice smooth swing—it looked no different than his dozens of swings prior.

The crowd rose up, watching the flight of the ball toward left center field. It appeared to be deep enough for the runner at third to tag and score. But to the dismay of the Berrien Rebels and the jubilation of the GAC Spartans, the ball disappeared over the outfield fence. Tears of joy streamed down Marc and Leah O'Brien's faces as the other parents pulled them into exuberant hugs.

While Jackson's teammates mauled him on the way back to the dugout, Marc made a phone call to his brother, Ned, in Duluth. Ned, a GAC board member and Jesse's other stepson, was sitting by his dad's bed, keeping watch. For the past two weeks, Jesse had been unresponsive, and the family knew that he would soon cross over to be with the Lord.

After receiving the exciting news, Ned leaned down close to Jesse's ear. "Daddy, Jackson just hit a home run," he told him. In amazement, Ned watched Jesse's eyes open and completely clear.

"That's wonderful," he said, in his distinct Southern drawl, then closed his eyes once more.

GAC went up by two runs on Jackson's memorable swing, and neither team scored in the remaining three innings. The Spartans would live to fight another day.

But Brother Jesse Long would never open his eyes again. He passed away peacefully with his loving family around him the very next evening.

Chapter 9

WAITING OUT THE STORM

Sleeping late can prove to be an athlete's worst enemy. Cliff and his coaching staff roused the boys from bed fairly early the next morning. A good breakfast at the hotel in Tifton and a late lunch would be perfect for the three o'clock game time.

Cliff anxiously watched the radar report on his phone. "Bad weather is coming in around four o'clock," he told the other coaches. "It would be to our advantage to move the game up an hour or two." The Berrien coach, however, proved to be an immovable rock. Three o'clock was nonnegotiable. He mentioned something about testing and wouldn't budge.

Anyone with a computer could watch the progress of the incoming storm. Fifteen miles away, Metter High School and Wesleyan started at two o'clock and got their game in. Meanwhile, the coaches and field crew at Berrien were still piddling around on the field. The actual first pitch was not thrown until thirty-five minutes past the scheduled game time. It was a clear signal of gamesmanship.

The Spartans had won the coin toss and were the home team. They held the Rebels to one run in the top of the first and promptly began pounding their opposition like a drum. Up 5–1 with no outs, the rain began to fall. When lightning streaked the sky, the Spartans were sent to their minibuses and the fans scattered to their cars.

At five o'clock, the game was cancelled and both coaches, after looking at the weather forecast for Thursday, made the decision to play the deciding game on Friday. That only meant that Berrien could and *would* bring back their ace pitcher who had been victorious in game one. Coaches Shelton and Schofield drove the two buses back to Atlanta that night, fighting a relentless thunderstorm—more than four nerve-wracking hours.

When Cliff got home late that night, I questioned him about the start time of the game. "Surely that coach was stalling for a rain out." I was agitated thinking about five Spartan runs down the drain.

Although it had been a long two days, I was surprised to hear my husband give the Berrien coach the benefit of the doubt. Cliff never once griped about the adverse circumstances his team was facing, stating that it would just be a waste of his energy. The humility of this man was truly inspiring. I desperately needed some of his humble spirit to rub off on me.

The next day at practice, Cliff pulled Jackson into a hug and told him how sorry he was about the passing of his grandfather. "I understand if you don't want to play tomorrow," he told him.

Jackson looked his coach squarely in the eye. "No, Coach, I want to play. This will be the first game my granddad gets to see me play this year."

Kathy Sisco, our athletic department secretary tried to charter a bus so Cliff wouldn't have to drive the team back down to Nashville on Friday. When no charters were available in the Atlanta area, our athletic director, Dr. Tim Vick, insisted on driving one of our school buses for the team. Even though our boys' and girls' soccer teams were playing for a state championship that evening, Tim wanted to support and serve his longtime friend. I promptly found a seat on the bus with twenty-one players and four other coaches in order to avoid the long drive. The hours flew by as Cliff entertained us with humorous baseball stories from his long coaching career.

As I finished setting up the video camera behind home plate, I was shocked to see Brother Jesse's wife, Marilyn, sitting with her family in the stands. Jesse had passed away less than two days prior, yet here she sat ready to cheer on her grandson and his team. It's where Jesse would've been if he could've.

I immediately went to her and wrapped my arms around her in a lingering embrace. "Jesse was so good to the Sheltons," I told her.

She responded affectionately. "Jesse loved the Sheltons."

Despite her loss, she continued to accept hugs and greet everyone with her characteristic upbeat attitude. I couldn't imagine how hard this must have been for her.

When the Rebels' ace took the mound, he appeared to be pitching as hard as before and with great determination. Our boys, on the other hand, were too anxious. They helped him out during the first two innings by swinging at bad pitches.

Cliff recalled his first state championship series in 1987, wishing he had made his boys take a strike before swinging the bat in game three. He didn't make his team take a strike this time but told them to make their pitcher work—control was going to be an issue with only two days' rest.

Down 1–0 in the bottom of the third inning, the Spartans tied it with one and then added three more in the next inning. By the time we chased their ace off the mound, the score was 6–1.

Our defense was stingier than Scrooge. Senior outfielder Connor Joseph made a spectacular diving catch in foul territory, and junior, left-hander Peyton McGuire pitched a complete game jewel on the mound.

When the final out was made, Jackson O'Brien doubled over and began to sob. He had repressed his emotions long enough. Coach Shelton immediately draped his arm around him, feeling the same powerful combination of grief and joy. Life and baseball suddenly meshed together in a conglomerate of triumph and tragedy.

With tears still fresh on his cheeks, Jackson trailed his teammates across the infield, shaking hands with the crestfallen Rebels. Berrien's gracious announcer in the press box congratulated our boys for their 8–1 victory. He sincerely wished them all the best in the semifinals against, none other than, Westminster—our region's top team.

Meanwhile, the Spartans rushed to left field jumping around, throwing their arms over their heads, yelling, "AH! AH! AH!" in unison. This had been their victory chant for the past month. The lively celebration was in no way disrespectful to the Berrien crowd. This undistinguished, number four seed had every right to whoop it up. Everyone who knew the story of this team and their coach couldn't help but feel some of their unbridled exuberance.

The boys eventually trickled off the field into the arms of their enthusiastic parents and girlfriends. When Coach Shelton stepped around the backside of the dugout, he was surprised that Marilyn Long was waiting for him. She threw her arms around his neck and pulled him tight. "Oh, Cliff," she breathed with tears clouding her eyes. "Jesse loved you so much."

Cliff swallowed hard, staving off a wave of emotions. "I loved him too."

It was a tender, unexpected moment. Both of them knew that when this season ended, the bond between Jesse, Cliff, and baseball would be over. But oh, what a meaningful fellowship it had been!

Chapter 10

FAMILIAR FOE

May 19, 2014

Three days later, on Monday afternoon, the Spartans only had to travel twenty-two miles into Atlanta to take on the Westminster Wildcats. This series would mark the fifth time our two teams had battled one another this season. Although the Wildcats were the region champions and the number one ranked team in the state, incredibly, the Spartans had little fear of their semifinal opponent. The teams had split during the regular season—two games apiece.

The Wildcats state playoff victories had been jaw-dropping. They were perhaps the most powerful hitting team in the state, averaging eleven runs per game. They had outscored their opponents in the first three rounds of the playoffs 65–10 without losing a game.

Prior to the start of the first game of the doubleheader, Cliff stood outside the dugout watching the Wildcats go through their pregame warm-up. He began surveying his opponent at every position. The realization that not one of his players could've broken into the Wildcats' lineup, save Division I pitching prospect Justin Lewis, was mind-boggling. The Spartans were a bunch of everyday, hardworking players.

Devin Daugherty, at catcher, hadn't secured a full-time position until his senior year. He was now throwing out speedy base runners every game and periodically stroking balls over the fence.

Junior first baseman, Harrison Kerr, had told Coach Schofield at the beginning of the season that he thought he was going to get cut in tryouts. When he settled into his position at first base, he began making incredibly athletic saves for his fellow infielders. Not only that, he was the heart and guts of the team, a fierce and fiery competitor.

Wade Cox was our steady, quiet, second baseman. He had been an unknown factor at the beginning of the season—he hadn't played baseball in eighteen months after suffering shoulder problems his sophomore year.

Junior shortstop, Lucas Boudreau, had been a starter on the JV the year before along with Doug DeBoer, who held down third base when Justin was pitching. Together they gobbled up every ground ball hit to the left side of the infield.

In the outfield, senior Connor Joseph, the fastest player on the team and Gwinnett County's leading base-stealer, tracked down nearly every ball hit into left. It had taken him all the way up to the state playoffs to settle into the starting lineup and hold on to his position. After Senior Night, he never came out of a game again.

In center field, Ross Wood had been a four-year starter, although his number one sport was on the gridiron. He already had a scholarship to play football at Dartmouth. Ross had never played on a GAC baseball team that had ever made it past the first round of the state playoffs. A righty hitting left-handed, he was now challenging for the season doubles record.

Right field had seen action from three different players most of the season until junior Peyton McGuire nailed it down. He had started there his sophomore year but shared the position early this season while trying to find his rhythm at the plate. When he was pitching, Will Lovett played a solid right field.

The Spartans' bats had gradually come alive as the season progressed, boosting their confidence along the way. Designated hitter Jackson O'Brien exuded poise through every at bat. He was a patient hitter with a good eye for the perfect pitch. Every time he came to the plate, he drew a cross in the dirt with the knob of his bat before stepping into the batter's box. He left no doubt where his confidence was coming from.

Cliff had fought hard to keep one of his seniors, Javy Lopez, in the baseball program all four years. While other coaches were unsure about keeping him, Cliff's heart went out to the big kid who looked more like a football linebacker. Baseball was in Javy's blood—his father was Javier Lopez, Major League catcher and Braves Hall of Famer. Cliff had a special place in his heart for the soft-spoken Javy, not because his dad had been a professional player, but because he was a genuinely selfless kid. Javy came off the bench in many games as a pinch hitter driving in numerous runs throughout the season.

And on the mound, the Spartans were not only riding the arm of Justin Lewis but carrying a host of hardworking pitchers who combined to win some great games throughout the playoffs. Ben Childers, Jack McLaughlin, Carter Willyerd, Adam Nakada, Peyton McGuire, Wes Bucher, and Brian Syphoe all started and closed games throughout the season. No one in the bullpen was an outright superstar, but when they were pitching well, they were more than capable of getting the job done. Hunter McKernan, Will Davies and

Andrew Schultz rounded out the Spartans' roster, unselfishly playing backup positions.

All in all, the Spartans were a blue-collar crew—ordinary baseball players playing above average—tall enough to be a decent basketball team, and with hearts the size of Georgia. They were a united team having the time of their lives. Many of the boys remarked that this was the most fun they'd ever had playing baseball. Coach Shelton quipped, "It's fun to take an average team and watch them do something well above average…so much more fun than watching a good team underachieve."

With a huge crowd in attendance, the red and gold finally had enough fans to make some noise. *Lucky* pineapples lined the roof of the Wildcats' dugout while the LACE cookbook held a place of prominence in the Spartans'. When the dust cleared on the first game, the boys of GAC relaxed behind a solid and surprising 5–1 victory. Justin Lewis had pitched a beauty, pumping his fist from the mound as the last out was put away.

If the Westminster Wildcats had been shocked by the Spartans' victory, it didn't take long for it to wear off. The first game only appeared to be a wake-up call. In game two of the doubleheader, their bats finally came to life as they ran through three different Spartan pitchers. Wes Bucher pitched hard in relief, striking out five batters, but the giant was fully awake and would not be denied. It was dark by the time Coach Shelton met with his team in right field to evaluate their 12–4 loss.

"Believe it or not," he told his boys, "we have momentum going into game three tomorrow. They made some sloppy mistakes at the end of this game—a couple of base-running blunders and some infield errors that showed a lack of concentration. We can use that to our advantage."

While the Spartans were downtrodden, they knew they had at least one more day of fight left in them. Earlier,

Harrison Kerr had walked by the backstop after shaking hands with the Wildcats and turned his gaze toward me from the other side of the fence. "Tomorrow," he vowed, eyes ablaze. "Tomorrow!" He exuded such determination and confidence I couldn't help but feel a glimmer of hope.

As Cliff walked away from the huddle, he heard his warriors stack it up and yell, "WFC!" That chant had propelled them all the way to the Final Four—*What a way to go out*, he thought.

Chapter 11

THE HAND OF GOD

The next morning Cliff and I stood in front of the mirror getting ready for school. "I'm tired of making these speeches to my boys at the end of the season," he said woefully.

Cliff can sometimes be *the glass is half empty* kind of guy while I am almost annoyingly the eternal optimist. Normally, I would've spouted all sorts of Pollyannaish sayings, but not today.

Today I had to face the harsh reality that this was the end of a great and unexpected run. "I know. That's the hardest part for me too," I told him.

I spent the rest of the day praying for God to give my husband the words he needed at the end of the game. Paradoxically, I also prayed for a win, just like I'd been doing since he lost his coaching position.

Praying for God to give our teams a win was uncharacteristic of either one of us. Somehow, we didn't believe that the God of the universe put much stock in wins and losses on the field and in the gym. But this season had changed my mind. I believed that God wanted to vindicate Cliff for all that he had been through. Most of the people I talked to were praying the same thing—for the Spartans to win it all. When all was said and done, wouldn't that show our administration that they had made the wrong decision? I struggled with such selfish thoughts day after day.

There was one man at our school who had been walking this journey with us as if he were a part of our family. Of course, in our spiritual family he is our brother. Dana Davis had been a boys and girls basketball coach at GAC starting in 1981 and had finally retired from all coaching this year. He was a longtime assistant principal and math teacher as well. Dana had even been Cliff's first assistant baseball coach. Before our children came along, he and his wife, Susan, would sometimes show up at our house in the evening to play cards. Cliff and I taught all three of the Davis children over the years.

Dana is sometimes referred to as "the prophet" of GAC. Everyone knows him as a mighty man of prayer and vision. He has undergone an incredible transformation in his life, from an overly competitive coach, to a wise, mission-minded servant of God. Much of that transformation is a direct result of a devastating diagnosis he received in 2000 of multiple myeloma, a cancer formed by malignant plasma cells. It is considered to be incurable.

Many patients diagnosed with multiple myeloma have three to seven years to live. Dana has been through two extremely painful stem-cell transplants but has continued to travel all over the world in various mission efforts. He lives life to the fullest, knowing he's on borrowed time—the way we should all live.

In 2013, Dana appeared to be losing his battle with cancer until he was put into a small group of patients at Emory Hospital in Atlanta and given an experimental drug. With literally hundreds of people all over the world praying for Dana, he received the news in 2014 that his disease was in complete remission. His doctors were exhilarated over his response to the new treatment while the rest of us were praising God for His benevolence on Dana's behalf.

Dana's perspective on sports and winning is one that Cliff and I have embraced fully. Years ago, Dana sent our entire coaching staff a message with the following words: "Though he's my friend, I fear telling my athletic director I have not helped my players become better athletes. But I fear this more: standing before Jesus trying to explain why I neglected all the opportunities I had to lead my players to Him. I tell you, all our trophies will be rubbish on that day. He tells us we can't serve two masters, yet I fear we try. May God help us."

Having a man like Dana praying fervently for the baseball team to win the state championship was impactful to say the least. Now I turned around to see Dana in the stands at Westminster giving me a giddy thumbs-up. I knew what he was thinking; I knew what he was praying—I was too!

This game was also being played at the same time as the visitation for our brother Jesse Long. Someone asked his wife, Marilyn, about having to make a decision between going to the visitation or the game. "Well, you know where Jesse would be," she replied. "He'd be at the game."

The Spartans had won the earlier coin toss, and Coach Shelton promptly sent our closing pitcher out to the mound. Senior left-hander Ben Childers had only started two other games this season and had never thrown more than four innings in a row. He wasn't a hard-throwing pitcher, but he usually had good control, worked fast, and kept the ball around the strike zone. Today, our closer was going up against the Herculean Wildcat hitters. They could smell blood in the water.

When the fifth inning rolled around, Ben was still on the mound. He hadn't struck anyone out, had walked four batters, and given up only three hits. The Spartans' defense had been spectacular behind him. They had already turned two of their eventual three double plays.

In the third inning, Wade Cox, at second, had picked up a ball that careened off the glove of Boudreau at shortstop and threw it home to nail a Wildcat runner sliding in. Connor Joseph had been playing deep left field but made an incredible diving catch just behind our shortstop. While the Spartans played the field in the top of the fifth, catcher Devin Daugherty picked off the Wildcat's first baseman, who had taken too big of a lead at second base. As the game progressed, the Spartans played loose and fearless while the Wildcats pressed and took ill-advised chances.

The score remained 0–0 until the bottom of the fifth inning. Wade Cox came to the plate for the Spartans, flying out to center field. Next up, Lucas Boudreau was promptly thumped in the arm with a pitch. He trotted down to first base without flinching. Harrison Kerr headed back to the dugout aggravated when he struck out looking.

With two outs, Jackson O'Brien strode around the umpire, drew a cross in the dirt, and stepped into the batter's box. Strike one swinging. He stepped out of the box and studied the end of his bat.

"Foul ball," the umpire called on the next pitch.

With two strikes on the batter, Cliff looked across the infield and took off his cap, a sign to Coach Schofield to send Boudreau on the next pitch. He briefly studied the note card nestled within the lining of his cap. That card had been there for many seasons as a reminder that he was not the one in control. "Many are the plans in a person's heart," it read, "but it is the Lord's purpose that prevails" (Proverbs 19:21).

As the Wildcat pitcher started his motion toward the plate, Lucas took off from first. The crowd came to life as

Jackson sent a towering shot toward the right-field corner. The Wildcats' right fielder sprinted to catch the ball, but it landed just out of his reach no more than an inch or two inside the foul line in the very corner of the field.

Had Lucas not been running on the pitch, he would've been thrown out at home. As it was, he dove in headfirst, sweeping his left hand across the plate under the tag. The roar of the GAC fans was deafening! Jackson saluted his teammates from second base but could not score as Justin Lewis made the third out of the inning.

In the top of the sixth inning, a bad feeling swept through our crowd. Westminster now had runners on first and second with only one out. Everyone knew the floodgates could open at any moment. The next batter hit a scorcher on the ground toward third. Justin gloved it, tagged the bag at third, and threw a bullet to Kerr at first. Double play—inning over!

Without scoring in the bottom of the sixth, the Spartans now had to do the unthinkable—hold the Wildcats to a scoreless game. A quiet and determined Childers headed back out to the mound. His opponents had not been patient at the plate all day—he was banking on that to continue in the seventh.

The Westminster field is not a big one, nestled down along the banks of Nancy Creek, which has been known to flood the field on more than one occasion. To keep the balls inside the park, a massive green wall stands on the right side of the outfield. The first batter of the inning, #23, was at the plate and had already watched two balls go by. On the next pitch, he sent a ball to deep right field, well over the head of Peyton McGuire. Peyton jumped up against the green wall with no chance of catching the ball, which had hit near the very top and was now bouncing back into right field.

The batter hesitated slightly rounding second base, then promptly ran through his coach's stop sign. Meanwhile,

Peyton barehanded the ball and threw a one-bouncer straight across the field to Justin Lewis at third. It could've gone either way, but the umpire knew as well as everyone else on the field that #23 should've stopped at second base. He pumped his fist aggressively toward the player in the dirt.

"YOU'RE OUT!"

Justin leapt in the air with passionate enthusiasm. He knew the moment he put his glove down that the runner was out. He excitedly ran the ball over to Childers on the mound amidst thundering applause.

As long as I live, I'll never be able to explain the chills I felt during that last inning. Later, others in the stands would describe the same sensation. I knew the Spirit was moving on the field that day. It felt like the hand of God—there was no other way to describe it. When our boys made the final two outs—a ground ball to second and a pop-up to short—tears spilled down my cheeks unashamedly. I left the video camera running at the backstop, climbed up on a chair at the railing behind me, and was enveloped in the arms of Robin Lewis, Justin's mom. We held each other for a long moment, crying and praising God.

The video camera, completely unattended now, would record one of the most poignant scenes of the season. After the Spartans finished their celebration on the infield, Cliff was still standing in close proximity to first base. One-by-one, all nine of his seniors sought him out on the field, enfolding their coach in a heartfelt embrace.

And for the first time, when the Spartans ran into right field to celebrate the victory, there was a white-haired man jumping around in the midst of them, throwing his arms in the air yelling, "AH! AH! AH!"

It was the perfect speech at the end of the game.

♦♦♦

With the sun setting behind them, the team gathered in closely for a photo on the field, proudly holding the cookbook above their heads. They were a dirty, scraggly looking crew, all pointing toward the cookbook, save for Ross Wood on one knee, dead center, pointing toward the crowd. If it hadn't been for the facial hair of Connor, Lucas, and Harrison, you might've thought it was a bunch of exuberant little boys. Their joy was contagious.

As the field cleared, Jackson, along with many of his teammates, made their way back to Campus Church of Christ to pay their respects to his grandfather, Jesse Long. Still wearing their dirt-stained uniforms, they hugged each family member expressing their sympathy. Many at the visitation were moved by their thoughtful devotion after the game…a bittersweet moment for Jackson and his family.

Chapter 12

CHANGE OF HEART

That evening I drove back home heady with victory. So many GAC supporters had been at the game, many of them in attendance not because they cared about baseball, but because they cared about Cliff. The Providence coach, Adam Cantrell, and his young son had placed their lawn chairs right next to the dugout. After the game, someone asked me about the man cheering wildly near the fence. Adam still possessed the fire and passion of a true sports competitor—tonight, he was a devoted Spartans fan. He wanted this victory as much as his mentor did.

All along the way, Cliff continued to receive messages from his opponents—texts and emails—wishing him luck. Even the other coaches in our region wanted him to know they were behind him. After tonight, GAC was the last baseball team out of twenty-three high schools in Gwinnett County still in the state playoffs. Now, even the county schools desired a state championship for the Spartans. They wanted one of their most respected baseball coaches to go out on top.

An email message caught my attention as I waited for my husband to get home. Cliff and Gary Schofield were the other two recipients. It was from Dana Davis—his words were piercing and needed.

> *I am just praising God…and as I thank Him, He reveals Himself.*
>
> *Cliff shared of a man whose heart is softening, Gary shared a text from a rival school, Adam (Cantrell) shared his love for Cliff…and we see clearly that as Jesus shines as Light before men, people see good and God receives glory.*
>
> *But the main thing impressed on me as I drove home was that we are to love…that is what God desires most. And (this is not natural for anyone) you are to especially love those who mistreated you…those who fired you.*
>
> *I had to write this before it becomes less urgent in my feeble mind…cause I'm pretty sure it came from God's mind (which is never, ever feeble:)*
>
> *Love you all…and 'Congratulations!'*
>
> *Dana*

Something changed in all three of us after that message. I realized I had not been walking the road of humility—I was still harboring uncharacteristic feelings of anger and resentment. It was ungodly to say the least. The next morning, I wrote to Dana.

> *You are so right…actually, God is so right! I have forgiven those who did this but I do not love them the way I should. Please pray that I can love the way Jesus does.*

He is a God of justice and desires justice for His children. I believe He is bringing about that justice through these warriors on the field. It's time for us to love without reservations. Thank you!

Gary spoke with Cliff the next morning. "I've been convicted in my heart to love *our administrators*." He mentioned them by name. He told his good friend that he was going to make it right. Later that morning, Gary sat down with one of the administrators and told him he loved him. Although he was still upset about the decision that had been made, he was determined to love the way Jesus loved. Gary used the word *agape*, not meaning brotherly love but a Greek word meaning self-sacrifice, wanting the best for the other person. Both men wept.

Cliff too was convicted. He came home Thursday after practice and asked me to read a message he was sending to each of his administrators. Exactly thirty-two years ago we had interviewed for jobs with two of these men. They were the ones who hired us and had supported us all throughout our teaching careers. It had seemed so strange to be at odds with them now.

Even though we were trying to get ready for high school graduation, Cliff didn't want to wait. "I need to send it now," he said with an urgency that claimed my full attention. He apologized to his bosses for harboring ill feelings over the past month and wanted them to know that that was no longer the case. He told them he loved them and was praying for them every day. Little did they know, Cliff had been praying for them by name every day for many years.

The manner in which my husband handled himself in this very public situation had been admirable. He was asked on a daily basis about his circumstances, yet he never once demeaned our school or administrators. He would usually smile and say, "God is in control. It's all good."

A month ago, Cliff had been read a list of reasons why the school wanted to find a new coach. While his athletic director and longtime friend, Tim Vick, had fought for Cliff throughout the process, he had not been able to prevent the final outcome. Knowing how devastated Cliff would be, Tim wanted to be the one to tell him the hard news alone. As painful as that had been for both men, Cliff's first words to his good friend were, "I'm sorry you had to do that." I readily admit those would not have been my first words.

It felt like an emotional burden had been lifted as the coaches now prepared the Spartans for their final opponent. God was granted full permission to carry the entire load. It brought about a much-needed peace before a championship series that would push the resolve and integrity of our team and fans to the very limits.

Chapter 13

STATE FINALS

Benedictine Military School, Savannah, Georgia
Saturday, May 24, 2014

The Spartans' charter bus to Savannah left after practice on Friday afternoon. It was carrying the coaching staff and twenty-one players, nine of whom had graduated from high school the night before. While the road warriors were headed south, I drove to the Atlanta airport to pick up our twenty-four-year-old daughter, Alex, who was in graduate school at the University of Central Arkansas. As the two of us hugged in the airport, we felt each other's excitement over our final baseball road trip together.

Alex and I have enjoyed a close relationship since she was a little girl. I consider it one of the greatest blessings in my life to have been able to coach my own daughter. Not many women get to do that. She was my starting setter her junior and senior year on the varsity volleyball team—a tireless bundle of energy with an unquenchable passion for the game. Alex's teammates used to laugh at her bicycle kicks after a hard-fought point. Her sophomore year, she was a backup setter to one of my seniors. She got to play in about a third of the matches that season. Instead of asking me at home about playing time, she would come to me afterward to say, "Thanks, Mom, for letting me play tonight!" I've always cherished her grateful attitude.

Saturday morning, mother and daughter got up early to begin the four-hour drive. Arriving at Benedictine over an hour before game time, we wondered if there was another event going on other than the baseball game. Cars lined both sides of the road long before we approached the parking lot. The tailgating festivities were comparable to that of a college football game. I felt lucky to even find a parking place near the field. Soon we realized all of those cars were here for the championship series.

The all-boys Catholic school Benedictine Military School was founded in 1902. There is perhaps no other school in the state of Georgia that can rival their alumni following. It seemed that anyone still alive who had graduated from Benedictine was in attendance at today's doubleheader. No bleachers were left open for the visiting fans. Bleacher seats filled every inch, even if no one was sitting in them. Lawn chairs surrounded the backstop, sometimes four or five chairs deep. Nearly all of the area around the outfield fence was already taken up with canopy tents and lawn chairs. Our players' parents found a spot to squeeze in a couple of canopies in deep right field—too far away for the Spartans to hear anyone cheering for them.

Every decent filming location was already taken. Alex and I finally decided on a set of tall bleachers turned backward facing the football practice field down the right field line. It was not an ideal angle, but there was no other choice. Even setting up the camera in the top corner of the bleachers brought rude comments from the high school students who had climbed to the top row to watch the game over the railing. The atmosphere was hostile; you could feel the tension in the air before the game ever started.

HONOR ON THE LINE

Prior to the game, Coach Shelton was told by the Benedictine coaching staff to have his team lined up on the first-base line. The color guard was going to walk onto the infield for the playing of the National Anthem. Cliff was specifically told not to let his team leave the line until the flag had gotten off the field.

When the color guard exited through the outfield gate, the Benedictine coaches went inside their dugout. The Cadets, however, remained on the third-base line staring at our players. The GAC coaches also left the line, then wondered why the Spartans had not followed.

Unknown to Coach Shelton and his staff, the Wesleyan players, who had lost to Benedictine earlier in the week, had told our guys to hold the line—the Benedictine players prided themselves in being last on the line. Even when the pregame music blared across the field and the Cadets' pitcher started warming up on the mound, the Spartans held. So did the Cadets.

Finally, Cliff realized what was going on and told his team to get in the dugout. As soon as they walked off the line, the Benedictine players clapped and yelled at our boys as the stands erupted. The Spartans walked into the dugout amidst a storm of ridicule.

We were now facing the last of the number one teams in the state. Benedictine had polished off two other opponents from our region—Lovett in round three and Wesleyan in round four. Today they were facing the fourth-ranked team out of our region for the ultimate prize in high school baseball. No one would've dared to dream such an unlikely scenario a month ago.

Justin Lewis gave up six hits in that first game, walked one, and struck out three. The GAC defense made the Cadets pay for even thinking about taking an extra base. The second inning ended with one of their runners getting picked off at third.

In the top of the fifth, neither team had scored until Connor Joseph homered to put the Spartans up 1–0. But in the bottom of that same inning, Justin hit the first batter, who ended up scoring on his teammate's double. The seventh inning would tell the tale.

When Ross Wood came to the plate, he led off with a double to center field. Alex let out a piercing scream as Ross nearly got picked off rounding second. His helmet flew off, and he picked it up off the ground while scrambling safely back to the base. I could see that wily grin on his face...even from a distance.

Connor Joseph was up next, but the Benedictine pitcher wasn't going to make the same mistake against him twice. Connor ended up flying out to the second baseman.

The unobtrusive Wade Cox stepped to the plate. His strength all season had been in the field, playing a nearly flawless second base. He'd only committed five errors in thirty-four games. The Cadets had little to worry about from Cox. To that point, he only had eighteen hits, all singles with the exception of one double.

The Benedictine hurler only threw one ball to Cox, a pitch he would've taken back in a heartbeat. He stood helpless on the mound as the ball took flight over the left field fence—a two-run homer that would be the game-winning hit! The GAC fans cheered their hearts out from deep right field, barely audible on the infield. Wade rounded third, giving his beloved coach a fist bump, and headed for home. His teammates were waiting with open arms while a silent, edgy crowd watched from behind the fence.

After Justin caught a pop-up in foul territory to end the game, I felt a little uneasy about our surroundings. Many of the fans had been consuming alcohol prior to the game. The students standing all along the outfield fence and in the stands where we were filming had been spouting vile epithets toward our players all throughout the contest. More than once I had to tell Alex to let it go. She was ready to give them a piece of her mind. I could just see the headlines in the *Savannah Morning News*: "Coach's wife and daughter caught up in state championship bleacher brawl."

Fortunately, just before that game had started, a group of men, all Benedictine alumni from thirty years ago, surrounded the two of us at the top of the backward stands. Even though their language was a bit salty at times, they provided a buffer zone around us. When they found out we were Coach Shelton's wife and daughter, a friendly banter commenced, and we were saved from the unruly teenagers. One of the men returned to stand beside us all throughout the second game. It was obvious he intended to protect us. There was honor in the ranks after all.

Game two did not go the Spartan's way from the first pitch to the last. The Cadets were already up three runs in the first inning before junior pitcher Brian Syphoe came in to relieve a struggling Peyton McGuire. Peyton was met by tremendous heckling as he jogged into right field. He would have to endure the cruel taunts the rest of the game. He did so with class, ignoring the verbal abuse and playing flawless outfield.

This was Brian's first chance to toe the rubber in the state playoffs. He got us out of the first inning and held the Cadets scoreless in the second and fourth, but home-run balls proved his nemesis. Benedictine hit two in the third and one in the fifth. Even so, the Spartans continued to play stellar defense. Connor Joseph threw out a runner from the outfield, and Devin Daugherty threw out a base-stealer at third.

A bright spot in the 7–2 loss was the pitching performance by Carter Willyerd. The senior pitcher held up his end of the bargain. He controlled the sixth and seventh innings, allowing no runs, walking one, and striking out one.

With a split, Coach Shelton and his team were destined to stay in Savannah the rest of the weekend. The Georgia High School Association prohibits sporting events on Sundays, which meant the Spartans would be spending two more nights in a hotel in downtown Savannah. Not an ideal situation, but not a bad one either. Savannah is known for its Southern hospitality—great accommodations, incredible restaurants, and plenty of historical scenery.

While we would not have chosen to lose that second game, it set up what would become one of the most moving experiences of Coach Shelton's baseball career. Had there been a sweep by either team, that Sunday morning in Savannah would have never taken place.

Many of the boys will not understand the extraordinary significance of that Sunday morning until they are men. But to those of us who have experienced the magnificence and adversity of what life has to offer, it will always be treasured as a sacred moment—a beautiful picture of the life to come.

Chapter 14

BIGGER THAN BASEBALL

On Sunday morning, the team gathered in a meeting room off of the hotel lobby. Coach Shelton thoughtfully regarded his twenty-one boys, seated around long tables in the shape of a horseshoe. They weren't really boys anymore—they were battle-tested young men, accustomed to having their backs against the wall.

Alex and I were invited to join in. We sat at the far side of the room feeling privileged to be a part of their devotional service. The team spent more than an hour together around the tables, much longer than their coaches had planned. But the Spirit was moving that morning in a hotel in downtown Savannah.

The staff's first-year coach, Garrett Granberg, was giving an inspiring lesson. "There are over five hundred high schools in the state of Georgia with roughly nine thousand baseball players at the beginning of the season. Now there are twelve teams left in all classifications, two hundred forty guys still out there playing." He paused to let that reality sink in—the fact that they were now only one of two teams left in their classification.

"This will be known as one of the greatest teams in the history of baseball at our school," he said. "Tomorrow you'll be playing in front of one of the largest crowds ever assembled at a high school baseball game in Georgia."

You could feel the sense of mission among the players. Every eye was riveted on the young pitching coach as he paced back and forth between the tables.

"Tomorrow night the season is over," he declared. "Everyone will go their separate ways." There was no going any farther. They had defied all odds and gone the distance.

"What things will you take with you from this program that are *bigger* than baseball?" he asked. And then he shared his favorite scripture from Romans 8:28. "And we know that in all things God works for the good of those who love him, who have been called according to his purpose."

At that point, the young coach shared a deeply personal chapter in his life. A chapter that included expulsion from high school, losing a full-ride scholarship to play football at the United States Military Academy, and ending up at Wheaton College playing football for a Division III school. His fate had been changed in the blink of an eye by a poor decision. But looking back on it now, God used those hardships in his life for good. He shared what the Wheaton College coach had told him in their very first meeting together. "The three most important decisions you'll ever make in your life are the decision to follow Christ, who you will marry, and where you choose to go to college." That meeting changed the course of Garrett's life.

After relating his story, Coach Granberg brought up some of the difficult situations their team had endured this season. Coach Shelton's dismissal from coaching was his headliner. He then caught the team off guard by mentioning individual players by name. These were players who had experienced notable failures but later came back strong to help the team win. There was a bit of good-natured snickering around the room while embarrassing moments were rehashed and owned by each young man.

"Peyton McGuire—you misplayed a ball in game two at Jefferson in the seventh inning causing us to have to go extra innings, but," he countered, "in game three at Westminster you played a ball perfectly off the wall and threw the runner out at third for the first out of the seventh inning." Peyton half grinned as the team gave him affirming nods.

"Ben Childers—when we played Westminster in the regular season, you were sent in with GAC up 7–5 and blew the win." Ben's chin dropped toward his chest. "But in game three against Westminster in the semis, you pitched a complete game shutout to take us to the state championship." A murmur of approval from the other players brought Ben's head up with dignity.

"Connor Joseph—the season in general for you was up and down; you were in and out of the lineup. But you've been in the lineup throughout the state playoffs, making an unbelievable diving catch on the warning track at Jefferson and hitting two big home runs in the playoffs.

"Jackson O'Brien—many unfortunate events happened to you during this season, including the loss of your granddad, Jesse Long." Jackson pressed his lips together and made eye contact with Coach Granberg. He knew what else was coming. "You hurt your arm, lost your catcher's position, and got mono. But you knocked the game-winning home run at Berrien to go up 6–4 and the game-winning double in the fifth inning at Westminster to score our only run.

"Seniors, you'll be leaving GAC. Everyone has a chance to write their own story, influence other people for the better, and do great things. Understand, there is a bigger plan. You may not see it, but remember, all things work together for good to those who love God."

He glanced over his shoulder at Cliff and then back at the team. "In the game tomorrow, play loose and have fun. Enjoy the experience. Play for each other, the program, and for your coach."

Garrett told the team that each one would now have an opportunity to tell one favorite memory of the season and say one thing to Coach Shelton. Nearly every player talked about the relationships they shared on this team. A couple of them said you usually have this kind of brotherhood bond in football not baseball, but they definitely felt it on this team. Many of them mentioned the team's turnaround and joked about the cookbook, but none of them mentioned their own accomplishments—it was all about their love for each other.

When they talked about Coach Shelton, every player had something different to say:

You've taught me how to persevere through hard things.

I watched the way you handled yourself through all of this, and you've taught me humility.

You've always been so positive with us, even when we were down, sometimes a lot. But you encouraged us not to give up. You never got mad at an umpire's call—always kept your cool.

You taught me what a true Christian looks like. You are the best example of a Christian man I have ever known.

I learned from you how to serve and think about others first.

You never took credit for anything—you always deflected it to the team.

I admire how you kept your sense of humor through everything.

When it was Coach Schofield's turn, he locked eyes with his good friend. "You made my life better. You didn't let me stay the same; you helped me be a better Christian." Gary went on to say that in high school it's easy to have a lot of friends, but when you're older and get married and have children you kind of lose what it means to have a friend. "But Cliff is a true friend," he expressed.

Cliff stood at the front of the room humbly taking it all in. He and his team and coaching staff shared a complex and personal relationship. They were bound by the fact that tomorrow would be the final inning—there would never be another. They had made it here on sheer determination—a run for the championship borne out of heartache and disappointment. He was grateful for every single man in this room and the bond they would share forever.

Clearing his throat, Coach Shelton thanked them for their kind words and told them he loved them. Then he pointed to the bread and cups of grape juice sitting at the end of the table. He told them, "The only reason why baseball is meaningful is because of this—because of what Jesus did for us." He read a scripture from the book of Romans and emphasized the sacrifice that was made for each one of us.

All heads bowed as Cliff prayed fervently that each one of these young men would be a follower of Christ. And then the band of brothers and their coaches participated in the one act that would unify them above all others—they took communion together, remembering the body and blood of Christ given on their behalf. There could be nothing meaningful in life apart from this.

Chapter 15

A DAY TO REMEMBER

Monday, May 26, 2014

The championship game time was set for 1:30 p.m. Rain clouds threatened the Memorial Day sky. I'm an early riser so I let Alex sleep in and headed down to breakfast. Cliff and Gary were already in the hotel lobby hanging out in a couple of comfortable chairs. I sat down across from them to see how they were doing. To be honest, I don't think either one of them had gotten much sleep in the last three nights—it had been a long weekend. They were both unusually quiet.

"What would you do today if you knew you couldn't fail?" I asked them.

Gary answered immediately. "If I knew we were going to win, I'd relax."

For Gary, that would probably be impossible. He was the kind of guy whose motor was cranking hard all the time. He could definitely get wound up and blow a gasket every now and then. Earlier this season, Justin Lewis hit what he thought was a home run and started trotting down the baseline. When the ball pinged the bottom of the fence, he took off at a sprint and was nearly thrown out at second. As first-base coach, Gary asked the field umpire for a time-out—unheard of if your player isn't hurt. He marched out to Justin, who stood sheepishly on second base, crossed his arms over his chest, and scowled at him. After several long seconds the umpire called out, "Coach, you can't just call time-out to stare at your player." Never speaking a word, Gary gave Justin one final glare, walked back to the first-base coach's box, and the game resumed. Justin never made that mistake again.

For the past two seasons, the coaches and players had been ribbing Coach Schofield about "the tooth." Gary had a temporary front tooth that could pop out if he wasn't careful. Earlier this season he got a permanent one, but up until then, he would be embarrassed for anyone to see him without it. Once, when Cliff and Gary were riding a rollercoaster on the freshman class trip in Florida, he lost the tooth while yelling. At the time, it wasn't very funny to be without his tooth on a class trip. Later, they would joke that "the tooth" was probably embedded in someone's forehead riding behind them. Gary even lost his tooth in a game last season when he adamantly disagreed with an umpire's call at first base to end the inning. As Coach Schofield was voicing his disapproval while walking back to the dugout, his tooth flew out somewhere around the pitcher's mound. I have him on video picking it up out of the grass. Luckily for the umpire, that got him to shut his mouth.

I could tell Gary was a little edgy, wondering how this day would unfold. I smiled at him and said, "Relax anyway; it's in God's hands." That was one thing both coaches could agree on. They trusted the outcome to God, either way.

When we got to the field around noon, it was raining. The team remained on the charter bus in the parking lot, preferring its comfortable seats to the visiting boys' locker room in the school gym. Tim Vick had called Benedictine's athletic director and asked them to provide space for the GAC fans. Alex and I were thankful to see yellow tape surrounding the bleachers on the right side of home plate reserving them for the visitors. That's where I would be filming today.

As we waited for the sky to clear, both of us enjoyed time under the umbrellas talking to many other Spartan fans. Some of them had stayed all weekend just to support Cliff and the team, including Sam and Patty Mankin with their grandson, Max.

The Sheltons go back a long way with the Mankins, thirty-two years to be exact. When we first came to GAC, Patty was one of the fourth-grade teachers, and I taught their son, Andy, and daughter, Ashley, in my PE classes. Both of their kids were special to me from the start. Andy eventually played baseball for Cliff all four years of high school. He was a sophomore outfielder on the 1987 team that missed the state championship by one out. Because of Andy's great sense of humor, Cliff would sometimes call him Uecker, referring to Bob Uecker, Major League baseball player turned sportscaster and comedian. The name stuck, and soon everyone on the team was calling him "Uke."

During Andy's senior year, he was batting .408 with seven home runs and 32 RBIs. He was a lefty, long-ball hitter, who happened to be the last batter for the Spartans during the 1989 state quarterfinals. He sent the ball for a ride. The center fielder for Bremen High School circled around behind the right fielder and snagged the ball, ending the Spartans' season. The next day at school, Dana Davis asked Patty how she was doing. She said she was having a hard day, but Dana had some surprising words for her. He told her it was good that Andy made the last out, because he would already be over it. Dana knew what was most important to Andy—baseball meant a lot, but his faith meant even more.

On a side note, Dana had been the disciplinarian in the junior high. Sometimes he would challenge the boys who were sent to his office to an arm-wrestling match. If they could beat him, they were off the hook. Since Dana was left-handed, he always put his left arm up on the desk. Andy Mankin was the only boy in junior high to ever get off the hook. Dana had forgotten that he was left-handed.

When Andy heard about the school dismissing Cliff from coaching, he sent him a letter from Nashville, Tennessee.

> *Coach Shelton, I just wanted you to know how much I respect you. My life as a Christian is better because of your influence. When my parents told me this was your final season as coach of the Spartans, I had many different emotions. I told my parents that their dream was for Ashley and I to go to GAC. They got to choose that, but God let me play for a fine Christian man. They could not have picked a better coach for me. Thank you for everything and God bless! Love, Andy "Uke" #18*

The 1989 Spartans' pinstriped jersey #18 was now getting drenched in the rain. Eleven-year-old Max Mankin, Andy's son, was standing in front of me, proudly wearing his dad's old jersey and red Spartans baseball cap. Max refused to stand under an umbrella. He had been in Savannah all weekend with his grandparents watching a high school baseball team battle for a state championship that his dad had played for twenty-five years earlier. Max's sandy blond hair and playful grin reminded me of Uke. The Mankins' presence at this the final game was meaningful in so many ways. It reiterated the true essence of Cliff's long coaching career. It had never really been about the wins and losses—it had been about relationships all along.

CHAMPIONSHIPS HAVE TO BE WON ON THEIR OWN

The weather didn't clear until late afternoon. Cliff walked to home plate for the pregame meeting with the umpires. When he reached for the Benedictine coach's hand, I snapped a quick picture. There are so many uncertainties in sports, but this was undeniably his last meeting at the plate as a coach. I wanted to document it. From his first pregame meeting to the last, he had preserved his humility and integrity. He was a gracious coach whom I admired greatly. We were the home team, winning yet another toss of the coin. At four o'clock, our boys finally sprinted onto the field—they had spent over three hours on the bus waiting for this moment.

I was strangely calm, crammed in the bleachers with a lot of rowdy GAC students, who had made the long drive for the final game. Alex stood beside me visibly anxious, desperately praying for her dad's success. As a coach, I normally get a premonition about the outcome of a game, but not today. I had no gut feeling either way. It's almost like the final result was immaterial—it was the journey to get here that had mattered the most. That still didn't stop my incessant prayers for Cliff and his boys. *Lord, help them honor You in the battle.*

Ben Childers determinedly took the mound. He gave up one run in the first inning while the Spartans took the lead in the bottom half scoring two. The Cadets added another run in the top of the fourth tying the score. The teams remained knotted at two apiece through the fifth inning.

There was a great deal of tension in the crowd. In front of our bleacher section were dozens of lawn chairs filled with restless Cadet fans—adults, no less, who should know better than to get into it with boisterous teenagers. But they couldn't help themselves. Every time Benedictine made a great play, some of the men would stand up and point at our kids, putting it in their faces. High school students have a difficult time letting that ride. Soon, things were being said and done that left little room for honor.

The air horn in our section was a particular annoyance to the Benedictine fans, and they sharply voiced their opinion about it. It didn't matter that the Cadets' fans were blowing air horns all around the field. Finally, I addressed our students, most of whom I had taught in elementary school. "Hey guys, let's just cheer for the Spartans; that's why we're here."

I was really proud of the attitude our kids displayed from that point on. They caused a mighty ruckus in the stands, but it was never again directed at the opposing crowd. The student with the air horn put it away, and in its absence, after every great play, a roaring chorus of, "AIR HORN, AIR HORN," rang out across the field. Now that's what I call clever, and perhaps more annoying than the actual horn itself!

Ben struck out the first batter in the sixth inning and gave up a solo home run to the next. After that, he grappled with the strike zone, walking two batters and hitting another. Cliff had to make a trip to the mound. Putting his hand on Ben's shoulder, he told him, "You did the best you could. Let's see if someone else can finish this up." Disheartened, Ben walked back to the dugout covering his mouth with his glove. He had so longed to finish this game the way he had at Westminster.

It took two more pitchers to get the last two outs. Senior Jack McLaughlin finally shut the door on the sixth inning, but a lot of damage had been done, and the Spartans trailed the Cadets 7–2.

It was sometime before the seventh inning that Alex went missing. I scoured the bleachers, but she was nowhere in sight—she had slipped away without a word. Finally, I caught a glimpse of her red hair behind the Spartans' dugout. She was pacing and sobbing. I quickly looked away, fighting back a wave of emotion. I couldn't afford to give up hope during our last at bat.

A scene from *Angels in the Outfield* played through my mind. Young Roger tells Al, the angel, "I'm glad you're here! I was afraid no one was going to show up today, since everybody knows about the angels." Al turns a sympathetic expression toward Roger. "No one's coming," he says. "Championships have to be won on their own. It's a rule."

Unable to give up my role as Pollyanna, I knew we could win…angels or not. McLaughlin held the Cadets scoreless in the top of the seventh, but the Spartans made two quick outs in the bottom half of the inning. When Javy Lopez scorched a single into center field, I told myself, *It's not over, it's not over.* Holding the camera steady on the next batter, I ventured a glance at my husband standing in the third-base coach's box. The expression beneath the bill of his cap was one of resignation. I knew exactly what he was thinking—*It just wasn't meant to be.* My heart was crushed for him.

More than anything, I'd love to finish this story with the cliché happy ending—the Spartans miraculously come from behind, celebrate their coach's first and *only* state championship, then carry him off the field on their shoulders. That would be the Hollywood way. But the final inning was scripted in agony and disappointment for nine seniors who had hoped to hand their beloved coach his first championship trophy. It seemed like God was conveying a message to Cliff: "If I give you this earthly prize now, you'll miss the whole point of your career. It's never been about the winning—it's always been about relationships."

When the last out was made, hundreds of teenagers burst through the outfield gate and stormed the field. That wasn't supposed to happen—fans were not allowed on the field. Obviously, someone stopped guarding the gate or just wasn't strong enough to hold back the tidal wave.

Cliff was trapped near the Benedictine dugout, unable to get across the infield to his boys. He watched the mayhem for a moment, then looked away. A couple of opposing coaches extended their hand to him and he graciously accepted. Finally, he began a slow walk around home plate, picking up his player's bat still lying in the dirt.

A young coach emerged from the dugout meeting his dad on the field with open arms. Shuddering through a sob, I watched Ty and Cliff share a long, heartfelt embrace. No longer the little boy huddled in a corner of the dugout crying, Ty met his dad man to man, sharing his pain, helping him swallow the bitter pill. Neither one spoke.

After the two teams crisscrossed the infield shaking hands, I made my way to the dugout gate with a line of somber parents trailing behind. Alex was already there; she melted into my arms. A man blocked the gate to the field telling us no one was allowed to enter. "I'm sorry," I said with as much respect as I could muster, "but that's my husband out there, and those are our boys. We're going onto that field." Thankfully, he stepped aside and we solemnly made our way toward the dejected huddle in right field.

All nine seniors were crying, some sobbing, as Cliff consoled his crushed warriors. He moved among them, tugging each one into his arms. Though he couldn't say anything that would ease their momentary pain, he wanted them to know their coach cared for them deeply. He couldn't really tell them that he didn't *need* a state championship—such a disclosure would've made their valiant efforts seem pointless. He was deeply proud of every one of his players and wished wholeheartedly that they could've pulled it off for themselves.

I put my hand on Cliff's back and he turned around, hugging me to his chest. "I'm sorry," I said, finding it hard to say anything else.

"It's all right," he said quietly. "It just wasn't meant to be."

There was a time early in Cliff's career when he would've traded all of his wins for one state championship. That was certainly not the case now. He didn't need a trophy to cap off this glorious ride—he only needed these young men by his side.

Cliff knelt down in the grass on the front row for a team picture. He and Wade Cox draped their arms around each other's shoulders. The second baseman briefly laid his hand on top of his coach's head, giving it an affectionate shake. They held each other's gaze for a moment while Cliff straightened his cap, then turned their faces back toward the camera.

"Thank you for an unbelievable season," Wade wrote to Coach Shelton a few days later. "It was the most memorable season I have ever been a part of. Thank you for not only teaching me baseball but also teaching me to be a person of character. At the beginning of the year you told us that the season should not be about wins and losses, but the relationships we make. Lucky for us, we experienced both. You have a great legacy, and I will always remember this season. It was unforgettable going to battle in the playoffs with you and the team. Thank you for everything you have done. Sincerely, Wade Cox."

Later that night, the charter bus carrying the worn-out warriors pulled into the parking lot at GAC. It was pouring rain. Time and weather meant nothing to the Spartans—they had plans. Just before midnight, the team gathered on the other side of campus. They wanted to see their field one last time—together. After tonight, their heroic journey would come to an end, but not before the cookbook was laid to rest.

Thankfully, the idea of burning the cookbook had come to naught; it was raining too hard. Instead, using their bare hands, they dug as deep as they possibly could into the hallowed ground outside of center field. The famous cookbook would lie in a shallow grave at the base of the flagpole. Water dripping off their faces, they shared a few words, hugged fiercely, and parted ways, leaving their memorable journey on the field.

Two days after returning home, Alex sent me a text message. She had been reading the book *Sacred Influence* and came across these words from John Adams, written to his wife, Abigail, during the Revolutionary War. Adams wrote, "We can't guarantee success in this war, but we can do something better. We can deserve it."

Alex insightfully connected those words to her dad. "It makes me feel a little better after thinking on it," she wrote, "because all along I believed he was deserving of a win, like it was owed to him. But the way he carried himself was deserving; it creates a different perspective and speaks even more to his character."

It also spoke to the character and integrity of his 2014 Spartans. Even though they were never guaranteed success, they deserved it.

The game of life, as in baseball, has always been fraught with tragedies and triumphs. Often, both are out of our control. We do well to leave it in the hands of God and engineer the one thing we can control—our own behavior. And in that final inning, success will be well deserved.

The godly walk with integrity; blessed are their children who follow them.
Proverbs 20:7

2014 SPARTANS BASEBALL ROSTER

Seniors

22 Ben Childers
5 Devin Daugherty
33 Connor Joseph
21 Justin Lewis
24 Javy Lopez
12 Jack McLaughlin
18 Jackson O'Brien
19 Carter Willyerd
4 Ross Wood

Juniors

6 Lucas Boudreau
27 Wes Bucher
3 Wade Cox
8 Will Davies
20 Doug DeBoer
7 Harrison Kerr
2 Will Lovett
9 Peyton McGuire
16 Hunter McKernan
13 Adam Nakada
11 Brian Syphoe

Sophomores

17 Andrew Schultz

Coaches

Cliff Shelton
Gary Schofield
Garrett Granberg
Ty Shelton

AFTERWORD

Sometimes God puts a word on my heart for other people. I've been known to pray that particular word over a dear friend or family member for months at a time. In January of 2014, I was prompted to pray the word *grace* over my husband. I asked God daily to show Cliff grace and give him graciousness in his life. At the time, I had no idea why the Spirit prompted me with that particular word, nor of its profound significance in his life during the months ahead. Looking back, I'm amazed at how God moves in our lives. He truly does work for the good of those who love Him. I believe my prayers for Cliff before his final baseball season were meant to shore him up during a difficult time. I've heard him say repeatedly, "I don't know how I did it." I know how. It was God's grace.

We will never be able to answer the question of why the state championship was so allusive…so many times. But I've found over the years that "why?" is rarely, if ever, the question that should be asked. Tony Dungy put it so well after losing the AFC Divisional game in 2005, just one more disappointment for him in a long line of disappointments. Coach Dungy said, "To me, that's one of the hardest things in life—what you hope for, and pray for, and dream about doesn't come true. That's when it's easy to get disappointed with God. Why didn't it pan out the way I thought it would?" But one of NFL's most respected coaches goes on to say, "It worked out the way God planned—not the way I had planned."

Five years later, as Cliff looks back on his long career and subsequent finish, God has given him a new and vivid perspective. Not one of regret or bitterness but one of thankfulness and appreciation for all that he has experienced and the lessons that he learned. And as a result, the *final inning* unexpectedly turned out to be a *new beginning.*

After thirty-two years of coaching baseball and teaching ninth-grade health, Cliff Shelton is now a sophomore Bible teacher and the associate athletic director at Greater Atlanta Christian School.

Made in the USA
Columbia, SC
28 September 2019